M000158913

STROLL ON
JAMES RUSSELL

Newton-le-Willows

Published in the United Kingdom in 2021
by The Knives Forks And Spoons Press,
51 Pipit Avenue,
Newton-le-Willows,
Merseyside,
WA12 9RG.

ISBN 978-1-912211-70-8

Supported using public funding by
LOTTERY FUNDED | ARTS COUNCIL ENGLAND

For Alec Newman

Contents

1. A "Retiredate"

"Doing anything nice this afternoon?" said as the dentist scrapes
Plaque from your teeth,
As the outlet of a water-hook gargles
On the floor of your mouth, as you hear him say, "bit of food here,"
And as you try and fail to say that you had a bowl of chilli
Con carne for lunch,
With the intonation of one of Nature's naughty boys. At such
A point you know how a Guy Fawkes in a wicker chair
Feels, immediately
Coming to mind that these stuffed figures don't figure in this modern world.
And if you are like the man in question – a long-toothed and suffering
Retiree or Retiredate (as he calls himself) – you will want to cast your eyes
To the hills from whence cometh
Whatever-it-was (he is or was a
Scientist, not a student of the world of imaginative words) and gain
That calm or balm; and you cast your eyes to the glaring eye of the
Dentist's light, above which you'll see
Emblazoned 'BELMONT'. Well,

Belmont was and is his name. His first name; which spurs the question:
Why?
One day in the early 1940s George Thom, an Army dispatch-rider,
And his ATS girlfriend, Brenda or "Bunny" Hawkins,
Were motor-biking en route to somewhere better
Than where they were and had reached
The outskirts of London, the south-west, near Sutton, also near Cheam,
When the bike broke down. George pushed the bike to a garage
In the nearest town or conurbation called Belmont. While the garage
Did its work they drank beer in the nearest pub and then made love
In the nearest field, thus kick-starting the man in question.
Of course they called him Belmont –
Belmont George Thom, whose story this is.

It will be told in a strange form or genre. You've heard
Of the prose-poem – a term about as descriptive as a proper name:
Poetic language set out like prose
Justified to the right in regimented paragraphs. Well …
This is written in *poem-prose*, being language that's prose
Or verging on prose,
But set out like a poem: with line breaks often for no good reason;
With each line beginning
With a capitalised word, for no good reason.
I say verging on prose. Sometimes it will be the flattest
Of discursive prose and sometimes it will relax into something that is
Itself. I warn there will be
Some higher waffle …
And rather than chapters there will be things that look
Like poems if you half-close your eyes.
You'll be able to keep up if you can
Be generous. Squint a little and don't worry
About the occasional eccentric of syntax.

2. Aqueous, Side-Burned, Constant Seething

Imagine you're a chemist, I mean a research scientist
Like Belmont was. Not the kind of chemist who serves
You with your Aqueous Cream;
And that you're able, almost casually over lunch in
College, to make a better fist of explaining what spacetime's all about
Than your Physicist colleague was
To somebody whose research field is Mallarmé.
And imagine too that a few months later you struggle
To explain osmosis to your twelve-year-old nephew
Because you're just *too tired*.
You wake up tired every day, fall asleep before documentaries
On, let's-say, yacht rock.
Belmont retired late because research grants
Kept him going and when he finally did go the ageing force crashed him
Over like a sudden breaker and shored him down.

Were these aches, that limp, that fading sight, this vagueness
In speech, this proper-name pathology where
You had to scratch out definite descriptions
In lieu of, say, Jeremy Paxman ('horse-faced has-been
One-nation Tory fly-fisher'),
There all along, ignored because work kept his mind
Away from them, or had a switch been thrown
Once he sat down on the fat cushion of his pension? The chemistry
Of it all, the medical chemistry bored him to tears. Who cares
Why the Xanotypan he took for his racing heart made him giddy
When combined with the Phelotanicon taken for his psoriasis?
As for the delta-spread from the gamma-inhibitors
That live in his glaucoma drops …
And don't start him on the dangerous liaisons of Nantosin, his blood
Pressure pills. He had become a new chemical ecosystem, whose

Governing brain longed to find out how things would go without
The intervening medications and the engineering:
Just stick to coffee and wine
And try a little *laissez faire*. Back to Nature, with death
As the major natural state.

Black humour didn't suit him.
But that's the suit he wore. Not black 'humour' in the other
Sense. He was Sanguine, Phlegmatic, and firmly
Of the view that ageing was not for him. He could accept
The bodily debacle, the mirror shouting
'complex medicine'. Being tired all the time is fine
if you seldom have somewhere you have to be. No.
His problem was this:
                    The cliché is that ageing is
A second childhood; but it's a second adolescence. Think

Of the adolescent triad: idealism;
Being eaten out with the injustice
Of the way things are in the peopled world … and
                    morbid self-consciousness.
The last one is the least obvious and so I'll start
With that (while all the time avoiding the taint of
Victorian arch, the teasing lecture and
Failed light touch of the side-burned
Children's author).

In the mid-teen mental house nothing is irrelevant
To oneself and this oneself is the pre-Copernican Earth.
What 'self'? It's a tender secret, private
As a dream,
Walled around by the familiar battlements: bozo,
Thinker, contrarian, blushing cringer.
Well, oldsters too – now I know some of this is as weak
As an adolescent essay written late on skunk –

Are divided selves. Okay, not swaddled babas inside a stockade,
But certainly a vital core of vigorous youth
With almost-erotic charm within
Those grim, strangled-by-certainty exteriors.
And as the mirror-image of adolescents' firm belief
That there are chinks in their armour through which their tender spirits
Can be glimpsed,
The oldster wants to let his inner 30-year-old *leak* out
Through twinkling eyes or a sparky turn of phrase
To certain attractive 30-year-olds, often professionals,
Like nurses, charity supplicants, those behind Post Office counters.
The direction of travel is different
But the principle's the same. Turning now

To Idealism … No, I don't mean nonagenarian ladies sitting
In their Albert Hall boxes with their dresses emblazoned
With the Swastika-like logo of Extinction Rebellion.
I mean the hyper-rational and simple, the unanchored and absolute
Radicalism of the retiree. Compare and contrast with
Its adolescent equivalent: the sixth-form agit prop.
(And even as I say this, the queasy shadow of a Moral Maze
Intro rises in the gullet; but I must go on …) Look at it

This way: when working they were behind windows
Misted up to hide the moral-political world
Flowing on
Without them. They stop working and the mist clears
For them, standing
In the open air to show a sparkling reality.
Here – a warm pint of beer is bicycled past village-green cricket
By a maiden aunt en route to church
And there – tubercular urchins are stuck up chimneys.
This 'open air', however, is not open air
But a vacuum to be filled by their ideas
On how things should be arranged. Ready they are

To fling their intuitions
Down a chute of verbiage
Towards a grateful nation.
In the Left corner they look for Nye Bevan
Quotes online and social-medially post them like warriors.
Where once the Welfare State was something
To take for granted or whinge about,
Now it's a religion and its cathedrals combined.
Their home-life is one of constant seething
Over the news, scorching
Themselves on blazing injustices. Seething too,

In the Right corner, will depend on education.
They may doze off over Michael Oakeshott or
They may foam over the mouthpiece
Of the social feeds, timidity matched
With killing words. In both cases
There is the adolescent clarity/certainty about
What's wrong
And what is to be done,
Scaffolded by and grounded in
'reasoned argument.'
If only they could sit down with the neo-Nazi psychopath
Or the vegan with the anti-Trump banner
And the love for George Monbiot
These people's prejudices would melt away, not *like* anything.
Just melt away. You see

Nothing mediates now between them and the political world.
They don't have the shell of work any more.
It's just them, their feelings, and the mess we're in,
Or not,
According to who you are. Let's stick with seething
As it's the bridge
Between idealism and what I called the state of being

'eaten out with the injustice
Of the way things are in the peopled world.' Consider

The fifteen-year-old spitting the word *stupid*
Under his breath at family gatherings and school assemblies.
'Rules? Who needs 'em,' as somebody once said.
Well, the adolescent oldster cringes seethingly when he thinks
About what people do now.
Of course, there are the common cases:
'Can I *get* a ... ?'
The N *Haitch* S
Walking out of shops without a glance
To the left or right
The screaming illogicality of the return
To the short-back-and-sides ...
Which stir only faint-because-common echoes.
No, consider a male (yes,
Yes, I know I know),
One evening at the theatre, sort-of enjoying
A well-carpentered play,
He descends to the toilets at the first interval
To find a long sullen queue for the Ladies and a door
Marked M but with
An inverted cross dangling from it
And an upwards arrow at the top-right,
Plus a crossed arrow at the top-left –
To cover all bases, he supposes, and why
Cover all bases?
Tentatively, he opens the door to hear, "Can you
Hang on a few minutes!" (A woman's voice from the stall).
He does. She brushes past in a leather coat.
Then upstairs to find his large glass of *Pino Gris*
Is warm and as welcoming as newly-passed urine. Now,
Do you think he could then go on to give a toss
About how Rattigan has decided to tie things up ... Consider

Watching a young couple eating
In the local café.
If the meal involves substances like mashed potato
Or crushed avocado
It's not unlikely that one of them
Will hold
The eating irons vertically like prison bars
And then do this: seeing that both fork and knife are overloaded,
Scape the contents
Of the knife onto the fork and then open wide –
One big chewfest! Done with one stone.
It's the scraping, the scraping, the doltish offering. Were
They never told off for doing that as kids! … kids …
Their ignored toddler watches the loved-ups
Forking food into each other's mouths … You must
Try this darling. The toddler cries; of course, of course.
And another thing do I hear someone say:

"Have you noticed that teaspoons are getting smaller?"
How the *hell*
Is one supposed to measure 5ml of a much needed
Medicament and cope with the sticky fingers
Under such CIRcumstances!

Remember Belmont? When young, he was shy and
Tall and big-about.
But compared to the modern bearded lumber-lout,
Who must have been weaned onto beef with beef sauce,
Who must have been lifting weights when others were
… Got the idea?
He is little indeed. Little in a corner, silent.
There's the lumber-lout scraping mash
Onto tines holding battlements of greasy pap. Examples
Could fill a book; but rendering it down: such an ancient adolescent

Surveys the new order and concludes either that here is
Stupidity, simple-as-that, or
That here we have the smarmy ignorant falsity
Of the tight-suited blade … "Enjoy the rest
Of your day." The sadness in all this occurs

When Belmont catches his own eye in a shop window.
Where there used to be happy blood and doughty phlegm,
Now there's 'yes-indeed' black bile in the set
Of his jaw,
In the cornered venom of his gaze,
Revealing in his stride
All the wrong kind of determination.
Determined for one thing to prove
That children now rule the world.
                    George Woodcock it was,
Once General Secretary
Of the Trades Unions Congress, who said (more
Or less): 'In general, I am opposed to generalisations;
Though of course this is a general statement'.
Exactly. Only one of these children
Who are erroneously assumed to rule the world
Would seriously believe that there is a deep
'In general' about the ado oldster
and that Belmont exemplifies it *tour court*.
And *does* the triad I mentioned capture some deep truth
About what sardonic old Belmont calls retiredates?
It all depends. While, like George, one admits
That this is 'all-depends' is a general statement,
Explicitly quantified universally. Yes,

Belmont knew plenty of men and women.
Some of them counted as friends
Around his own age who would stand

As 'ugly facts' against this 'beautiful theory.'
Benign contented people, laughing enthusiasts,
People who caught the latest films and read the latest
Novels, who were within themselves
Their real age, who thought
Laying down the law about worldly ways
Was for the birds and seethed in the proper service,
Not to the kind of modern deliverances sketched above.
While Belmont,
And some others,
Thought their agèd appearance was a lie;
And seethed and ejected
One-size-fits-all ideas onto the world
(Belmont's was not political, except for
The woeful absence of 'a scientific attitude'
In all domains); others tinkered
With ancient motorbikes, measured out their lives
By the classic dramatizings on Radio 4 Extra,
Treated their grandchildren and enjoyed not
Having to get up every day and go to work.

But Belmont's – let's be open and
Call it – misery
Was real.
His age squatted on him, was
A kind of spiritual tapeworm.
It will soon be time
to talk about his wife.

3. Bouts Brief and Long

How wonderful it would be to have a central organising
Principle, a sufficiency of belief, rather than this ferret-
Rich mentality.
                    What are dreams? Maybe they're
These insufficient ferrets manifest in dream-clothes
Acting out our turmoil between brief bouts
Of urination or duvet flinging off in a sweat from last night's
Surfeit. In one of his long bouts

Of unintended idealism, he would toy with the idea that nobody
Should be allowed to vote who could not make
A decent fist
Of saying what was The Periodic Table.
This wasn't chauvinism. It was
A boyish desire for order,
Not in politics but in the dream of a life
Threaded through with organising stuff-and-principles.
The Table is not a list of items in a car-boot sale,
Nor is it a plane of unique bagatelle pins to be negotiated
By the ball of life. It's the variety of manifestations of
Atomic structure. It has rationality, learnability,
Beauty. I won't
Go on,
Because in Belmont's scheme I would be denied the vote;
But it's enough to make the point that
He must have felt homeless to have thought this way.
Homeless in his beloved 'hard fact.' But
When all is said and done, there comes a time – going for
A third cliché? – when we (Belmont and ourselves)
Have to embrace a cooler sentiment, apricot
In flavour and looking like it would float. Solid

Failed ideas exactly determining the self by desires
Soon fly out the window and the sensibility
Of a labourer replaces encumbering scaffold.
If only this overheated cold man could have imagined
Himself as a cowboy riding the range in winter
And fitted some cooling sentences around the scene:
'As he passed there was a quick flurry of snow
And the flakes
Were welcomed as they cooled his face … '
The cowboy wasn't sure if he was the hunter or
The hunted but he had a job to do in that cold place
Which exhausted everything he had to think about.

4. Tuppence (in Old Pennies)

Belmont was old enough
To remember the comic Jimmy James, a teetotaller
And non-smoker whose act was to be a
Drunk with a fag on his lip, in evening dress with party
Streamers about his shoulders. He would pleadingly gaze
At the audience, blow smoke alternately from left and right sides
Of his mouth and say:
"Have you met the wife?" Belmont
Was not without humour, and there had been times
In the pub when he would take a mouthful of cigar smoke
And puff this to a friend in his best 'northern.'
But his hard dark imagination could picture the killing of the joke,
Or killing joke, when Tuppence Thom bounds
On stage calling the stage-drunk 'Old Poison' or another of her
Charming nick-names for him, telling him to get
On with preparing dinner because she was
Going out. If you were sitting at the back

Of the stalls you would see a bird-boned woman
Seeming about 40 with distinctive hair (depending on her
Latest spasm): jet-black bob, Monroe-blonde, flaming
Locks evoking Caitlin Thomas. And, equally distinctive clothes:
Short leather skirt, Celtic flows of fringed calico,
Severe business suit … and a *set* expression (even
From the back of the stalls). If you were in the front
Row or if – here's a chase to cut to – you were standing
As close to her as Jimmy 'Belmont' James, you'd
See an elderly woman trapped inside a carapace
Of tarnished youth.
Stilted, a photographed grimace, desperate.
Yes, indeed, Tuppence, his wife, was younger than Belmont:
But by little more than three years.
I'll do
            as I did before and begin with names and histories.

The eldest of Tuppence's siblings had been christened Penelope
And called Penny by her parents. As Tuppence is
One more penny than a penny, the second-born girl
Was called … that; and Lord knows she was no Penelope.
But a clever girl, she won a place at an ancient University
To read Natural Sciences, being tutored in Chemistry
By third-year postgraduate … Belmont Thom. It was
The mid nineteen-sixties.

5. The Lost Boy

They hit it off again and again in the beery summer
So thoroughly that Tuppence fell – that *is* the word –
Pregnant. Morning sickness
During her finals and then the plan
To terminate the pregnant state.
Time was tight; but when champagne's flowing
On a happy punt and your fingers are dangling
In the cool water, well frankly
Everything seems possible and nothing matters 'terribly.'
And then there is the cure for hangovers (more booze).
Upshots were an obscenity but there *was* one
And they missed the abortion window. It was
A different world then. My knowledge is slim
And I really can't say how it came about:
Their decision? *Her* decision? More likely than not
She felt a child would block the golden road opened
By her expected First, and adoption was agreed on. What

I do know is that in those days the to-be-adopted child was
Taken from the mother after a few breast-feeds and that
Was that.
She called him Junior; they both called him Junior; and he was
Small and frail with brown eyes like his dad's.
Sucking greedily and smiling in his sleep after the feed.
"It's wind," a mannish nurse explained. It wasn't. This nurse
Came in one morning and Junior was gone,
Along with his mother – long gone. But well within reach
Of the law's long arm. A petite pretty girl angrily smoking
Over a tiny baby in a waiting room at Kings Cross
Was apprehended and that was the last she saw of Junior.

Here the dawn of no faith, a sour item is revealed,
Blank arrangements. Still as a folded sheet on a high shelf,
Tuppence was unchanged on the surface but sometimes
The curtain parted to show the black caverns of her thought.
The first person singular
Referred now to her body only. 'How are you doing?'
May have well have been addressed politely to a tabby cat.
She got her First,
But a better word for it was her Last.
In those days Belmont's capacity for suffering
Was running on empty.
His capacity for empathy (as it was not called then)
Was an efficient reasoned thing. His capacity
For duty stood in an empty field waited to be saddled.
They married.

6. From Joblettes to The Dingle Players

Belmont worked. What else?
Tuppence did little more than call chemistry 'a bore',
It seemed every hour on the hour 'like a gong'.
What do you do when the tide and the fire have gone out?
What do you do when the covenant is a becalmed flag
And the landscape is a kind of Croydon.
Or, better, the Lincolnshire Wash punctuated with jet-planes?

In the landscape there were two toiling figures: Belmont
In the lab and lecture hall;
Tuppence is a series of joblettes with 'bores' as colleagues.
"Have you ever met somebody who's not a bore?"
Asked Belmont over dinner.
"You mean apart from you, darling, darling fascinator?"
Was the curdling reply.
The upshot was: she'd decided there were oceans
Between them and that she was joining an amateur dramatics
Group called The Dingle Players. Gawd 'elp us and lawks
A mercy.
She was cast as Sally Bowles and adopted the first of many
Severe black bobs.
She threw all she had
At it, which was almost nothing but enough,
And triumphed because not only had she discovered
A shamelessness, but there was something of Bowles
In her. Belmont fidgeted in his seat in a school
Hall with about thirty others wanting to stick
His fingers in his ears as she shrieked her numbers
And to block words overheard about the qualities of her
Exposed flesh. And so it continued: a sequence of triumphs
Within her sort-of imagination.

Belmont didn't mind.
He'd come to the pub after rehearsals finding
The Dingles to be quite down to earth (except for those
Who mouthed *tomorrow and tomorrow and tomorrow*
And *Goodnight sweet Prince*),
Silently wincing
Along with him as Tuppence held court at the other end
Of the table. This he could stand, while what he could not
Were the acid aftermaths of the Dingle theatre trips:
Trips to other am-drams, to professional productions.
He stayed away, but could not stay away from his own house
In which Tuppence held post-mortems over drinks –
Shopped for and mixed by her husband who, she said,
Was the owner
Of a cloth ear for dialogue and nuance.
The evenings descended into drunken banter, but before
They did she'd lacerated and patronised each show in her
Stage voice (an urgent shout). The nadir
Was, having fawned over him in a crush-bar somewhere,
She began to refer to the actor Mr Pickup as 'Ron.'
"Ron tells me he spent Easter in Seville," cut into
The usual silence of their dinner, cooked by Belmont
As she had lines to learn – Shakespeare Gawd 'elp
Us and lawks a mercy. Cleopatra she was –

A triumph of *unintended* comedy was this production.
Enobarbarus was played by a big-as-a-house retired copper.
His famous speech done in the mode of Crown Court evidence:
"I was proceeding in a north-easterly direction along the Nile bank
When a barge made of what appeared to be gold caught my attention.
I ascertained that it contained the defendant." What can an actor

Do when all about her (maids holding fans)
Are falling through corpsing ice, snorting with suppressed
Guffaws. When some of the audience are making a precipitous

And disgusted departure. What to do when the black rubber
Asp you are holding wiggles like a tadpole in your hand
And you need a prompt for what comes after 'Antony! Antony!'
Her black cartoon of Liz Taylor's eyes could not protect her
While she was all protection. Was it ferocious self-protection
That rendered her immune from the knowledge
Of her disaster, that framed it as slightly muted triumph?
She was emerging from the sea as a prize joke-butt,
But did her finest acting off-stage to hold her head up.
Or was it that after Junior she had no places left
Capable of being hurt. Her 'immersion' in the Bard
Had – she said – raised her mind to poetry,
And this was her next artistic campaign.

7. A Guide to Obsessive Forms

It's good to have a head start, having no ideas at all
And having one's emotions botched in a safe cemented
Under a rock pool. And so phrases bubbled shy
Of sentences judged on their prettiness and fitness
For rhyming and rhythming. She addressed herself
To the so-called obsessive forms: canzone, sestina
Villanelle – finding the repetition calming and a way
Of eking out her modest kitty. She applied

Her gifts for analysis and synthesis, still there
From her chemistry days, to other non (or less)
Obsessive forms – triolet, rondel, roundeau,
Roundel, ballade, and her beloved pantoum.
Haikus and clerihews eschewed.
She hammered away at sonnets sitting at her desk:
Tapping thumb, index, middle, ring, little fingers twice
To the addictive beat of what she called the "I-am-pen." Now

She served in her local deli strutting
With a ram-rod back, popular with those who did not
Know her. Not popular with her husband who still,
And nonetheless, hit it off with her until …
She became again a pregnant woman; but a different
Pregnant woman this time, as different as she was
From Belmont. Belmont was delighted, thinking
This could only do her good. He humoured her
To the point of agreeing to their calling the baby
Pantoum if a boy and, if a girl, Villanelle. The following
Could certainly NOT have been one of her Villanelles:

Here is a song we all know very well:
They took something impossible away
Welcome my darling daughter Villanelle.

Don't push me into saying all is well
Don't smile, don't be benign, just go away
And fill our coffers up with who-can-tell.

How can I speak of horror that befell!
My heart is brim-full of the who-can-say
My heart's a shop-full of nothing to sell.

My life's becalmed while yours runs on pell-mell
I make the beds and you make stolid hay
I do not breathe: gulp yawns and then expel

Against suburban lying I rebel
Spikes and specula on a hostess tray
Don't ever ask because you know damned well

Why I dance around this circle of hell
It's not my choice: it is the only way .
Here comes a song you'll soon know very well
Welcome my darling daughter Villanelle

8. Buttermilk or Killer Cowboys Bearing Down

No hot water and a table set with bananas, rye bread
And buttermilk; then early to a single bed to think on
Schemes for the betterment of mankind. That's not us.
It's not Tuppence. We don't live in the mountains;
But neither do we live in the valleys of scrub where killer
Cowboys, all in physical filth, dip
Their biscuits in the pork fat. Their specialist
Subjects being rot-gut brandy and whores. Tuppence,
At least, is in a different landscape along with some of us.
In it there is a someone small and speechless,
Almost abandoned on a shingle beach in the paltry shade
Of a kiosk back-grounded by a hotchpotch
Of Victorian villas. You could put this little someone
(a "she") within a wave's reach and see her so surprised
To be so buffeted. Some of them need a lot of love,
It turns out.

      For the putative mother of the little she, despite
Her loud shouts and efforts to beguile, there was
An infinite penumbra of ignorance about a solid
Core of knowledge proved by a certificate dead
In an unopenable drawer. For her there were
Only the following kinds of birds: eagles, seagulls, pigeons
Dickie-birds and vultures. With all trees being of one kind
Varying in appearance: likewise, for flowers. And up on
The higher reaches of ignorance there was a fabled twin vision.
On vision number one what lay before her was an attractive text
That meandered in garden paths, never quite or never
Reaching the fruition of meaning but clearly about
Whatever its *it's* and *which's* and *that's*
Referred to. She felt that if she paid the right kind

Of attention for long enough something would appear
As simply as a stranger telling you the time, whilst knowing
All along this would never happen because
She was the stranger. On vision

Number two there was a large but finite number
Of vaguely lucid vignettes of her life unanchored, floating
Not in water but upon a network of fine threads as
A waving mesh.
She had it written on a postcard close to her heart
Some vague-but-lucid instructions on how to stand back
From these silver threads to see the pattern, and in un-readably
Small print: 'You'll never do it darling'.

As for the present of that past vignette, there was only
The landscape of the real on which her bearing up
Was as unlikely as Belmont
Coming back from the lab in a sombrero and Zapata moustache.
Instead, her belly bore down on her. Surely Junior was never
This kind of stone weight. There was a stillness, a glassy one
That could crack open without notice. Sometimes
In the middle of the night
She'd wake with, or was woken by, the thought that her play-act
Was killing her because she'd colluded in a murder in that
Tacky waiting room in Kings Cross as she smoked the last
Of her packet of ten *Richmond*. But this would come before
A kind of mental dawn, maybe at 2.30 AM, the dawn that loving
What was left was the tunnel out of this.

9. A May-Pole Called Medicine Ball

At dawn on the First of May Belmont watched the birth.
The head emerged propelled by Tuppence's imaginative swearing
But the shoulders stayed inside. Two midwives presided:
One to help the baby out, the other to calm the mother's
Fury. And then with a sudden twist and a scream
From the belly the shoulders came and what Belmont saw:
The head from the back (triangular) those shoulders (lumpish
Workmanlike); that was *his* head and *his* shoulders; this surely
Was his son, and *not* 'Pantoum' (his red line).
"It's a girl!" (the remainder had been a doddle).
How lovely the mistake, how lovely the perfect strong-round
Creature. What was left of Tuppence struggled to register
This big bundle while Belmont packed himself off
So Love Potion Number Nine could be allowed to flood
Mother and baby.

He was alone with his strange euphoric half-sleep,
Happy and confident, with Tuppence's swear-words ringing down
His mind. These words seemed to increase in volume when
He returned to find Tuppence coddling her hair and not
Cuddling the newborn. "If you've come to see The Medicine
Ball she's over there asleep." This was now her name
For her, marginally worse than the "Villanelle." Is there
Such a thing as bonding? Belmont knew when he could
See non-bonding: the dutiful hefting of the baby for a feed,
The dutiful meeting of their eyes as she looked up at her mother's
Lasting for as short a time as possible, the cool practical concerns
About her wellbeing and a terrifying absence of the mother's joy
In her.
It was the stupor of a dull Sunday afternoon in that room,
Not the anti-chamber to a life Belmont had yearned for. Why

Was she The Medicine Ball or Ball for short? It might help
To think back to the tadpole-asp wrigglings and strainings
Of Junior and his tininess, his acute vulnerability, his
Need of protection and set this against the pumped perfection
Of the girl, her size, her seeming complacency as she
Tucked her thumbs into her fingers as if to say 'I'm sorted
Now'. Her blue eyes were calm and content and she seemed
To lack the biological assertiveness of other babies. She was
Greedy and this was enough to inspire in Tuppence
Garbage Guts as a gay alternative to The Ball. There was no

Mitigation once they reached home and settled
Into their threesome. The very best that could be said,
But was not thought by Belmont, was
That Villanelle became a project for her mother.
The resemblance to her father was the red rag inspiring
A head-down charge against the very idea of her becoming
Another Bloody Scientist. In later months Tuppence
Would try lulling her to sleep with readings
Of *Endymion*. Chagall prints, not scenes from the *Magic
Roundabout*, were pinned her wall. She even tried
Singing Ornette Colman's tune 'Peace' as a lullaby
Alternative to Keats. For Belmont

There was no scope for musing and not the slightest
Hope of getting back to some raw state of animal
Grace. He was relieved when his wife took up
The theatre club again, if only to present herself
At their frequent soirees as the poetic entertainment –
Despite the rank unwelcome-ness of her material (to which
I will return). Her absence
In the evenings meant that he had Villy
To himself, that he could invent jokes to share,
Involving blowing raspberries and his pretending to fall over.
So easy it was to make her laugh and bubbles come

From her lips. And sometimes she could be fascinated
By watching how different things fell from Belmont's hands:
A sheet of paper versus a Lego brick, a ball of fluff versus
A pencil. She pursed her lips … "Why's The Ball still up!
Let me tell you how they were challenged by my latest work.
Do mix me a G&T darling." It's not hard to get the idea
And easy for me to make good now on my promise
To return to Tuppence's new poetic direction.

10. The Horror, The Horror ... *Areté*

She was in no state for carving predictable tum-tee-tums
And reversing herself into rhyme-spaces. She may have
Been reading Plath or at least some of Plath's still-tougher
More ragged sisters. May have;
But then she never actually read much verse.
Perhaps so many ideas that came to mind
Received a cold reception in that space that she set herself
To do the opposite of what she'd been doing. No, not God
Forbid, go back to science: I mean, to do the poetic equivalent
Of screaming.

        It would be, she thought, to patronise the reality
Of childbirth and child-care (her minimalist version), to *craft*
Accounts of this; and so the reader, or more likely the listener,
Was treated to the full-strength blood, tearing, agonising,
And sometimes faecal mess of the opening scene.
'Unmediated' was the word she used, but it was hardly that.
Some generously inventive moves there were explaining
Everything gorily. It would have made things simpler to have
Given Villanelle the role of The Enemy, but she held up her head
And strove for nuance. No nuance hovered, though, around
The hard fact that motherhood was stealing and somehow
Steeling herself. Meanwhile,

Ambition fermented towards the need to publish. The
World must know just how it was with her. It's often
Claimed that there are so many little magazines around
That every poem is publishable somewhere. Well,
Here was the living proof against that idea.
Mimeographed efforts mushroomed
But

They were assailed by submissions from the usual desperados;
And editors have to draw the line somewhere. "Why, oh why,"
She wailed, were 'Mother Corpse', 'Intercourse/Extracourse',
'I Used To Be Able To Think' and 'Round-Hard Succuba',
And the rest, always found beneath that line? Her Am-Dram
Chums suggested self-publishing, but they should have known
Her better. Never *Never!* ... this in her Cleopatra voice.
But surely
There must be small presses around, she decided to believe,
That took the view that magazine editors only published
Mates' work (it was a 'closed shop' ... a popular term in the very
Early seventies); but that somewhere out there
Must be small poetry publishers bold enough to nurture
Blushing genius. The 'bores' who she detested
Would have said: "You can prove any theory by looking
For evidence for it." And she did.

One day, leafing through a mag she'd picked up in
Better Books or *Compendium* she saw:

Areté Poetry Press ... We're always scouting for good new
Poets. All types considered. Why not drop us a line?

And an address in Bristol. As toddler Villy pulled herself
Up by Tuppence's jean leg asking, "Whahdoin?"
Her mother laboriously typed out a collection
That she called *Spores of Blood* and posted it off to
The Hartcliffe area of south Bristol. When Belmont

Read the reply that came a week later he bit his
Tongue. He could see it was a generic photocopied
Acceptance written by somebody who could not spell
'beguiling' and 'genre' and a few other words and who had
Original ideas about when sentences begin and end. 'We know

you share our content [*sic*] for vanity presses, so we do
not seek a publication fee. We do however
Expect poets to put in an order for .... [150 was scribbled
In] copies of .... [Sores [*sic*] of Blood scribbled in]. So please send
A cheque for ....[£1,498.50 neatly printed in] payable to
Mr Gary Stokes.'

They arrived – ISBN-less, misprint-rich,
Maybe costing about two pounds each to make, retailing –
Retailing! – for £9.99. No,

      don't run away
With the idea that Tuppence was a fool or a monster.
She only showed sham-pleasure at this faux-success, coolly
Deciding to play this round to the hilt, producing more
Product for *Areté,* for a while.

And she found delight in Villy more and more,
Who would toddle after her into the kitchen, gently
Turning down her dad's offer of a story from a book.
She didn't repetitively read the *Puffin Book of Children's
Verse* to her, as did so many of her friends to their
Little geniuses, knowing she preferred taking
The back off an old alarm-clock and rooting around.
She loved the word Mummy on her daughter's lips,
While all the time donating copies of *Spores of Blood,
Enigma Dreams* and *Frond 2* to any human owner
Of lungs and eyes.

      She discovered cut-ups, surrealism
And free-and-easy-automatic, and did versions of them
While Villy crayoned multi-coloured stripes onto cardboard discs,
Stuck a pencil in the middle and spun the top to make
The colours blur to grey. She'd recently

Finished typing up her latest, called *Dense Light,*
And had popped it into the post a few days before
To the Hartcliffe address. Villy was experimenting
Away with balancing. Pencils, rulers, straws …
Balance at their middle point
But spoons do not. It was so rare to see her frown
But frown she did as she capitulated to the fact
That a spoon *will* balance if you abandon the
Middle-balancing rule. Such a beautiful rule that she
Loved as some girls love *Sleeping Beauty*. Her face
Relaxed eventually and the telephone rang.

"Hello?"
"Ello? Is that Mrs Thumb? Tuppence Thumb?"
[Belmont was in the local at the quiz-night]
"Very good Belmont … How many pints have you had

                                        you monster?"

"Beg pardun?"
"OK darling, I've got the idea. What's up?"
"Eh?"
"Who are you?"
"I am callin' from Areet Poetry Press."
"Areet? Do you mean Areté?" A-R-E-T-E-acute
[long silence; TV on in the background, an older woman
                        and an older man grumbling at each other]
"I works for Mister Gary Croft
[audible woman: "GarAY yer tea's on the table. Fir fuck's sake."]
… of AreetAY publications."
[audible woman: "GarAY! Will you get off that phone. Yer dad
        gotta make a call. Fir fuck's sake Gar!"]
"Thing is, you firgot to put yer cheque in wiv yer manuscript

                                        Mrs Thumb.

Goodbye."

11. Given Away by Your "Do"

It's possible to think that in the patchwork landscape
Of a running on this is just a bad patch, to think that you are
A complex system and that minute changes in complex
Systems can wreak desperate alterations, so quick
On to the next patch; and then to stop to accept
The passing cloud of How do I do that? And it is as if

Someone speaks out of the cloud to tell you
That your second 'do' gives you away; and the voice gently
Insists that the patchwork is not an endless continuum.
You should abandon the picture you have of yourself
As an ant on a patchwork globe wondering which direction
Is due North so you can decide which way to trudge next,
Or rather grimly to know which direction is which line
Of futility. The whole picture is wrong because

there are no laid-out sequences. If you want
To enjoy the comfort of a spatial trope at all, it's
More like the top layer of a pile you've built yourself
In your insect endeavours, overtime in your personal dark.
The building being a blind thing done in dreamless sleep.
The work continues through every night till one night
It is as if a door was slammed hard right next to your bed
And you sit 'bolt' upright like a sensitive meerkat – as
In the case of Tuppence and the phone call. The slammed door
Sweats out, in an instant, difficult memories that smear
Themselves all over your Spanish breakfast of tomato pulp
Spread on toast, drizzled with olive oil and sprinkled with salt.
What you call your 'breakfast' is now a buoyant lie,
Because the difficult memories are more real than
The present traffic. What you cannot

      do and what Tuppence did not even think to do
Is to perform the mental parallel to smashing a Spanish guitar
Against a concrete bollard, as the first move in the game
Of moving on. She did not move. She dug in, bringing sinews
To bear against the phatic banalities (as she saw them)
Of her husband's take on what stared him in the face
When he merrily returned from *The Bag O'Nails*.

12. Ivor's Plum Tree

Belmont loved to read to Villy Ivor Cutler's *Meal One,*
In which a planted plum-stone grows up inside the house
Of a loved-up mother and son.
They were both drawn to it, for different reasons.
Villy, because here was the sight of Nature
Pushing her way into the cosy human world; she wasn't
A bully: just being herself.
Belmont, because here was the forceful revelation
Of a dyed-in fact, an old assertion
Of the problem growing up through the floor.
The standing tall of greedy white roots invading
And smashing the over-furnished parlour demanding
That he visualise and confront
A life invasion. Where plum-tree roots
Sucked up the jam from dishes, drank the cat's milk,
His wife drained the sap from their family tree –
The tree with three trunks under one roof.

Cutler had resolved it all
By having the boy's granny obliterate the event by turning
Back the hands of the clock and reversing time to shrink
Back the roots to the stone.
Waking from which the always-happy boy called down
To his playmate-mum for his breakfast, "Meal one!"
Oh dear, oh dear, oh very dear …
Neither of the scientists liked this one little bit.
Turning back time. If Belmont could have at that point
Turned *forward* time by something under twenty years
He would have caused a belly laugh in Villy with his
Exuberant burlesque of Cher's *If ah could turn back taham.*
Well, moves like this, reversing time and 'it was

Only a dream' were quite beside it all. What happened,
And was happening, still remains behind.
That it was done is irremovable:
Unablateable, that's what you are …
It was not an event but the element he lived in.
It would be easier if it (the distance between his wife
And him) were in the physical not the mental world.
If this distance had lived in the carpentered world
The real-world equivalent of a fairy-tale woodcutter
Could have been called in to chop it down.

13. Undermined by Wankers' Britain and Del Shannon's Egocentrism

So much for reality.
The appearance was as of a sort-of happy home: sardonic boffin,
Harmless prima donna, and little sweetheart.
That the sardonic boffin hardly felt at home there
Was neither here nor there.
The steel beam that supported it all was Villy needing her mum
And Tuppence needing this.
We now compress time,
If we can find haha wayhay,
To glimpse through the blur of the carriage window, how Villy
Filled the home with children as a smiling still point or
A Warhol with her factory of nippers, the glow of which
Spotlighted the harmless prima donna to her intense delight.
Then Villy's surely-emerging stone indifference
To the merely imagined and love of the engineered;
And finally Villy's transition to womanhood and the necessary
Mothering of this, followed by Villy's sailing away
To the world of science and boys.

What is psychological reality?
It can be dull when set out like case notes.
But in order for us to get back to the agèd Belmont with which I began
A bit more must be endured. As if to save

        herself from drowning in the still waters of
Empty evenings, with Belmont working upstairs and Villy
At yet another party, Tuppence accelerated her Arts Project.
She used her *Areté* books as a 'track record' when submitting
To poetry mags (three successes and a huge party thrown for each),
Called herself 'a published poet' as she began taking flute lessons

And painting de Kooning-esque abstracts. She dressed now
In costumes, not clothes, and her natural pushiness allowed
Her to take over whatever arty committees there were
On her narrow horizon. And this, I'm afraid, is the penultimate
Home strait to Belmont's *O me miserum*
With which we began …

Back now to the 'reality'
Of this portion's first line. Tuppence's Arts Project
Seemed, then, to Belmont (not quite suffering yet) not a love
Of the arts or even of the arty world but an avoidance
Of the reality thing.
She failed to embrace modern novels, and not only because
Her husband read them, but because they held the danger
Of being a slice of life: too real by half.
Politics lived in the bore-box along with all science; only
The arts pages of newspapers were read and the News
Snapped off.
Popularity bears the stain of social reality and social reality
Is still reality, so all art that could draw a crowd was condemned.
Serious music was only allowed if new, unpopular, and refractory;
All romantic music and most baroque was 'kitsch.'
TV was detested. Belmont

                        could cope with this. Belmont and Villy could cope
With this; but he failed to cope (his daughter was rarely at home)
With Tuppence's world backwashing into his own: the soirées
And the committee meetings, the little gatherings, the dreary gaggle.

The women who came were mostly pale Tuppences; the men
Seemed to be savouring the temptation to patronise him.
This brought out a mischief in Belmont …

One Saturday afternoon a meeting of the Film Festival Committee
Was to be held in their dining room. Tuppence was expected to sit

At the head of the table before a bookcase on which lay a book
That had been a birthday present to him called
WALKERS' BRITAIN, its spine of cream lettering on dark blue.
It was an easy matter for Belmont
To blue-ink around an N outlined in pencil on cream card
And stick it over the L on the spine.
The meeting finished and Tuppence came out to him
Reading in the garden. She was limp of sail.
"It seemed as if they were all sharing some private joke," she said.
Her husband gave himself away with an un-secret grin.
Three minutes after her return to the dining room
There was a scream. Fun for him at the time but everything
Deepened a level.

Later Belmont pretended to try
To redeem himself by joining in one of her musical evenings.
No, she didn't play the flute, which was 'not yet ready for the public'.
At these evenings people brought along a favourite piece on CD,
Played it and then said why they liked it. When it was Tuppence's
Turn she usually did this in the poetic mode. In passing,

        she had recently discovered Walt Whitman,
Whose poetry someone has described
As being what results when you don't want to take the trouble
To write prose (yes, yes … pots and kettles).
Where poetry is usually assumed to be more elevated than prose, this
Can be happy to be *less* elevated or indeed well below the prose level and this was
The welcoming pool into which she dived. She had ready a Whitmanesque
Address to Albert Ayler.

Belmont was playing his cards close to his chest and drinking whisky
While the rest were stuck on dry sherry and white wine; and his
Mien was serious and shyly awakening to the interest of each one.
Nobody could have predicted his choice:

You Never Talked About Me by Del Shannon ...

You were talking
To a guy named Jim
And the things that
You were telling him ...
You talked and talked so endlessly tears filled my eyes
I could not see.
But you never talked
About me honey
ABOUT MEEEEEEEE HONEY!

"I love," said Belmont, "the operatic passion in evidence here.
He rips out the bleeding egocentricity of his heart
And presents it to us. Come on you guys! How many of you
Think you can make these top notes ...
ABOUT MEEE-HE-HE-HE HONEY."
Well a few poor souls did try to join in with Belmont's mad shriek
And then there came his collapsing laugh: helpless choking, spluttering
Honking; and he staggered out the room.

She said she could forgive his drunkenness.
(He was not drunk.)
She never drank more than one small glass.
(How could she?)
But she said this and meant it:
"Why do you want to undermine me?"
She had a point ...
Belmont was not a magnanimous man; he didn't try reasoning
And he certainly tried no tenderness:
Just withdrew to the back of the class with the naughty boys.
And soon after, they ceased
To share a bed.

14: Suck your Scratchings!

She saw her project in the arts
As a classroom of inner-city kids released
Into a summer field.
It was hardly that …
But the narrow determined thing was quite the kids-field scenario
When set against her other, parallel project –
Her youthening project. Sister

Penny had died of cancer,
Her father was long dead,
And now her mother died (*all together now campers!*)
Leaving Tuppence her house and all of her money.
What do we do with all this money? is a lovely question,
Perhaps, but not when this husband and wife chew it over.
They could move said he.
What! And abandon her local weird celebrity …
'It's my bloody money' was the theme.

So, she would become a free-range patroness of the arts.
That decided, she went to get made up to go out.
Epiphany is not the word.
More a matter of horror naturally balancing her faint euphoria.

"Oh yes, this badly needs making up:
This lined, sagging object falling to dewlaps"
(this was rubbish, because she had aged well, kept her looks;
Though the liner on her wide-set eyes had grown so heavy
over time that here were two Cyclops trapped in a coal house).

Whatever it costs I will spend to make a braver face,
Brave enough to adorn the literature of:

The Tuppence Thom Prize for Something
The Tuppence Thom Something Workshop
The Tuppence Thom Writers' Retreat –
Somewhere Nice in the Country.

Tuppence would vanish for weeks on end, calling
The absences periods of adjustment or health spa sojourns,
Returning each time looking less like herself
And more like a cartoon of a surprised nobody. Meanwhile,
Their home filled up with supplicants, mostly young,
Mostly men, with amazing ideas in need of her money:
Money to write a play, to burnish a nearly complete
Sonnet sequence, to buy a synthesiser so 'Earth Music'
Could be composed on it, money for a research trip
To Ibiza to support a drug-novel project.
Stuff O' That Nature. She had

a coterie of mostly-camp young men who
Dubbed her 'TT.' One day she and these courtiers were
Supposedly discussing applications to the *Tuppence Thom Foundation*
When she caught sight of Belmont departing for the pub …
"Belmont dahling! What are you wearing? Do come heah!"
Belmont had recently bought a blouson the colour and almost
The material of billiard blaize and had set this off with
An old pair of needle-stripe jeans.
"Oh dahling!"
Then one courtier said: *sotto voce,* "More Bellboy than Belmont".
"BELLBOY. Exactly!" (TT)
"From now on you will be Bellboy.
Now off you go, Bellboy, to meet the other old men
In the pub. What are you having with your milk stout?
Nice game of dominos?
Oh, and be careful of your toothypegs. If you have pork scratchings
Suck them, remember. Don't crunch!
Ciao for now!"

And this is roughly where you came in.
And it is exactly where Old Poison (her later coining)
Was born.

15. Two Middling Smilers

It is difficult to warm to, but who can live without
The middle distance. To be immersed
In the horror (see immediately above) or joy (please
Be patient) of what's now in your face in space and time
Is surely the way to go. And it's good to dress yourself
By the distant light of far glory or far misery: they set
Your present style. But who could love the middle distance?
In space we trudge through it head-down, wrapped in memory
And goal-direction; in time it's a bore to think about.
But middle distance people

      who deliver little to your face and who hold no promise
Of goals, either fulfilled or trashed, can be surprisingly loveable.
Which brings me back to Villy. Villy instigated nothing and believed
Everybody. She went along with all, just as the middle distance fits
In between the here-and-now and the there-and-later. She
Fitted in to what people said by lacking sceptical parts. She fitted
In with a smile that was both beatific and private. Her mother
Irritated her while her father she adored, but each parent
Was equally calmed by the radiance of those blue eyes.
To gossip with her was impossible. All her judgements about
People were generous and high-toned; while her passion
Was for processes and structures. Physics, she adored.
But a total lack of ambition held her in the middle distance
In a middling post in the north of England as a
Happy foot-soldier. Happy too,

      with her husband Lee. Lee was a *bloke,*
With a tubular neck and tight curls that spilled over his brow
Like the shrubbery of rough neighbours over your garden wall.
What Lee did for a living was obscure and changeable. Villy

Had said he'd been a technician in her lab. But Lee said to Belmont,
"Tell you the truth Prof, I was more of a cleaner." Then the last time
They met he said, "Actually Prof I'm more of a pub florist these days."
He was from the east end of London but seemed to have
Lived in most places for short times. Lee had

A something – a Halloween pumpkin light, a permanent light
Of irony, of happy irony, that shone from eyes no less blue
Than his wife's. Everything he came across teetered him towards
A hilarity that he only just supressed. And yet he only laughed
At simple deliberate jokes, laughed wiping tears away. He was,
Like his wife, a smiler. Tuppence called them The Emojis.
He called them The Smileys.

16. Half-Loaded: Milky Sweet All-Day Breakfast

Smiley they call him
Smiley's his name
[Then something or other]
And girded with fame.
It's time to explain.

Having, in the mid 1950s, caved in to his parent's pleas,
Belmont had taken his younger brother to see
An Australian film called *Smiley,* whose theme-tune I
Sketched just now.
He had settled himself back for boredom. In fact
His brother was the bored one – kicking the back
Of the seat in front – while Belmont watched entranced.
Here was a kind of heaven: life about the sun.
Everything was either yellow (the sun, the boy-hero's hair)
Or blue (the sky, eyes) or red (the bike that the charming
Little tyke eventually saved up to buy). Every meal
Seemed to be a milky sweet breakfast outdoors.
The sun had scorched away all dirt and gloom.
The word 'bum'
Was bravely pronounced by the charming tyke
To his teacher in class – a clarion demand to strive
Towards the open-plan of the world portrayed. Belmont

        had never been asked to describe, in adult terms,
The feeling this film had given him. He would have said roughly this:
Like when you begin the first beer of the day around 4.30 pm
In a dim cool pub with your choice playing on the juke box
And a bright sun shining in through dark-wood chinks.
Not drunkenness, no … Something opening to
Light, a splendid apartment that you thought
Was a slummy cell. We turn now, in illustration,

To the words (lightly edited by me) of the dictation-speed-
Speaker and jazz fiend, Willis Conover:
You know the narrow time when veils dissolve
And disappear
The view is clear
      If you could stay half-loaded all the time
      If you could know all the time
These things you know
You can't sustain it though.
More flatly he went on to say (in some liner notes)
That it widens into drunkenness,
Adding 'too bad'. Yes, too bad. Too bad too
That the window is so narrow. But neither
Do orgasms last long and they remain popular.

These windows were afforded to the retiree, were sought
By Belmont more and more these days. He did not join
Any 'afternoon men.' His pub men were evening men,
After-dinner men, round-a-table-secretly-sated-with-one-another
Men, grumbling, and dredging up jokes. The late-afternoon glow
Had to be a solitary affair … so *The Bag O'Nails* had to be
Shunned. Suburbia was explored. This suburbia was the kind
That came into its own in summer: hazy, cars seemed to
Traverse it underwater; seeming was the order of the day.
Flowers cracked open behind privets. He turned

             a corner and there was *The Turk's Head,*
A kind of afterthought of a pub; it seemed quiet and quiet
It was. He took his pint to a corner table and opened
A book. He was nearly the only drinker.
Across from him, a guy in his early sixties, something
Between a retired beatnik and a stage-gypsy. Pale
Of skin, sunken of cheek, black of hair.
Neat black beard turning to grey,
His long fringed hair going the same way.

A brightly coloured neckerchief and a jacket of bold tweed
Finished with gratuitous little workings of leather.
He was kneading strips of *Digger* tobacco and feeding
The result into a hangdog pipe.
He set the pipe down on his table next to his matches.

Then a hard look at Belmont,
Pee-holes-in-the-snow eyes –
Not unfriendly, but blank.
Was this a challenge? … "Scuse me mate
Do you mind keeping an eye on my pint?
Just going outside for a smoke."
(Accent: Northern, North Western)
" … Happy to," said Belmont.

17. Talking 'bout My G ... um ... Generation

The way to be left alone,
Research has shown,
Is to don dark glasses and invite people into the room.
Being welcoming can be a way of saying:
If you really want to intrude
I'll irritate you with my social mood.
And so Belmont, being Belmont, when the Beatnik-Gypsy
Said, "Fancy a half in there, a thank-you half?"
After he had done two short stints of pint-watching,
Had the first thought that the B-G was really saying the above.
But his second thought came out as, "Cheers, thanks,"
And his third as:
"Actually, watched pints don't do very much, I find."
"Bit like watched kettles," said the Beatnik-Gypsy, " ... never boil."

Neither man *looked* as if he had a sense of humour:
The Beatnik-Gypsy too edgy cool, and Belmont
With his *o me miserum* glass surround; but they cracked
A laugh and opened a packet of crisps.
The Beatnik-Gypsy saw the book Belmont was reading
And he said he'd just read the author's latest: "bit over-rated."
And they talked about the author and shared a table,
Drinking till Belmont could see the wide sea of drunkenness beyond
The narrow river's mouth, stopping at two pints. Belmont

         had become unsociable of late; but this was an event
From a better life. They had acres of common ground. The Beatnik-Gypsy's
Register was so relaxed, his irony light and positive unlike the old
Sour sort ... But let's not get carried away.
The fact was that Belmont had enthusiasms – for entertainers, pop songs,
Plays, novels, public figures, places, old jokes, foods – that formed

A semi-conscious reservoir of joyfulness over which the years
Had poured cement
That cracked and crumbled away as these two chatted on.

The novel was about a music-hall performer, and from this they travelled
To Max Miller. While Belmont began to wonder if the Beatnik-Gypsy
Was too young for these memories, his thought was nipped in the bud
By the other saying:
"You know what?
My wife."
"Yes," [Belmont getting worried, but it was a Miller gag].
"My wife is so ugly
I'd rather take her with me than kiss her goodbye ... "
And somehow this lead to a song popularised by
Norman Wisdom and Billy Cotton being sung very quietly
By them.
You gotta get AHT (out)
Get AHT and abAHT
To see old London TAHN
My advice to you in go and have a look arAHND
Before they pull the whole place DAHN.

Belmont's enthusiasms were not necessarily for things he liked.
Often for things he liked to think about and maybe mimic.
Likewise the Beatnik-Gypsy,
Who fetched himself another pint while Belmont
Eked his out. Belmont asked his name.
"Pete."
"Just Pete?" [the new Belmont sharpness].
"Pete T ... um ... Townsend."
"I'm Keith. Keith M ... um ... Moon. Actually it's Belmont Thom."
"That's funnier," said Pete.

18. Belmont — Neither Tough Nor Devilishly Sly

His attention to himself had been interrupted
And the consistent eventfulness of the rivers flowing
Past him stilled by this friendship or incipient one.
Let's hear it for distorting mirrors ...
He'd swapped one (his wife's) for another (a pub man's)
But the latter smoothed the jagged contours and replaced
The boring folds with interesting flourishes ... And what

Did Pete actually do – with his country checks, his artist's hands,
His antique-dealer's kerchief and sideways takes? "I used to
Have a small-holding," he said, "supplying veg for school dinners,
Till the era of self-serve pizzas and chips put an end to that.
I sold up ... or out."
Conveyed to Tuppence, this led to her calling him Turnip
Townsend ... "Bellboy and Turnip. A song, a dance, a pint
Of wallop." Was

Pete's backstory nonsense? Proper school dinners had died
Long ago. But more's the point: Pete seemed to know
So much about the literary and broadcasting worlds. Belmont
Mentioned two authors in the same breath. "Of course
They share an agent," said Pete. Sold-up small-holder?
That this was not on Belmont's nelly
Counted for nothing. He could be
Charmless but effectual, most of his life the hardly-noticed
Competence of the closeted man, now here he was –
A kind of daisy, a daisy-believer taking his cue from his daughter
In her open-borders policy re all sentences. As this pushed against
The sour-puss of Tuppence, amused her and softened her,
She snapped off courtiers who would smirk "How's Turnip?"
At her husband. He'd been shanghaied into the black hole
Of Pete's charisma – if that's what it was.

As time went on they moved from (say) weighing
The anti-merits of Cheerful Charlie Chester against those of
Sir Gerald Nabarro, whilst comparing the latter to Dickens'
Major Josh Bagshot ('tough but devilishly sly'), to creative
Pursuits such as inventing lyrics to a 'rich kid's blues'
That had to contain the remembered refrain *I was so downhearted:*
Threw my drink across the lawn. As long as this continued (to
Hammer the point) Belmont didn't care or register that
There was something two-dimensional about Pete; and
Why did he always wear the same clothes and kerchief?
Peter gave nothing away
About his personal life, bar rare references to
'Her in the great indoors'.
He had endless curiosity about Belmont and his career that
Flattered away the curiositee's own curiosity,
That was nothing beside their nurturing chats. Belmont

Would now bring a cigar to join Pete
In his smokes outside. A typical meeting might begin
With a probe into what was, despite it all, *good* about
Kingsley Amis and end with a joint struggle
To recall the full lyrics to the song that went *Hup!*
Bubble bubble bubble bubble bubble bubble
Bubble pink champagne
Why oh why oh why did you ever try ...
GRANDMA'S BREW.

Much later Belmont would rue (when is this word ever
Not followed by ...) the day when it was flatish brown beer
That should not have been tried and tried. It was a very

                        very hot day and brains seemed to be melting
Inside skulls.
But that was no excuse for Belmont's sailing beyond
His two-pint barrier into the breakers of the wide sea

Of drunkenness that threw condoms and sewerage
At him. He was a creature of rock-pools that the
Retreating sea uncovered, not this ...
Beer can seem so cooling, even if it is heatening. Pete
May have asked how Tuppence's flute was coming along.
He may have probed the lack of comfort uncovered
When Belmont's wife came up.

Belmont's language was ugly and best left
To the imagination.
It spilled out:
Fury, not resentment,
Wild flailing words more than directed fury,
Expletives undeletable.

"But she's only fighting the aging process, Belmont –
Don't we all do that?
One day she'll relax into herself," said cool Pete.

"Don't be daft," [this was a new Belmont,
Though new only to his new friend].
"If she would age along with me Pete, I could bear her,
But with this, this
Bloody freak-show of a wife."
"Belmont, it's not Tuppence you're angry with:
It's with getting old yourself.
She reminds you of the horrors by trying and failing to mask it.
It's like Dorian Gray in reverse: a young face evoking
True age ... But there is something you can do.
Get younger!"
"Oh fu ... sorry Pete. This is serious."
"I AM serious. Read my book ... I mean [rapidly] a book
That I happen to have a copy of called
A Touch of Daniel by Peter Tinniswood.
I'll get you a large strong coffee and a cheese sarnie."

19. They Don't Chase Motorbikes Do They?

Of course, of course, there is a design flaw here.
Many readers will know what 'a touch of Daniel' meant
In this comic novel (by an author, that surprisingly
Belmont had never heard of, nor seen photos of):
Toothless codgers regrew their teeth, ear hair fell
Like snow when baby Daniel was touched. So this

                        sets things up in the most unsatisfactory way
Of slackening
Whatever narrative tension could have lain before us … But
Sometimes reality, broadly understood, is not an artist.
Get over it:
As the Corbyn t-shirt – mocked by the two men – announced.

Waking the next day full of shame, he ordered *Daniel*
As a sleepwalker,
Reading it a couple of days later.
Found himself waking up.
Few writers – was one of his thousand thoughts –
Have unlocked the comic potential of everyday food so well.
He read through a grin and immediately the next book
In the Brandon family trilogy. Yes, of course (re *Daniel*),
The seeds were sown, pretend seeds in pretend soil pretendingly,
In the hope that something-yet-to-be-determined
Would grow through the curtain.

Daniel the book buoyed him up, it buoyed *them* up. 'Old Poison'
Gave way to 'The Joker' …
Tuppence had been complaining about two bickering women
On one of her countless committees. "The only advantage,"
Ground out Belmont as Uncle Mort, "that women have over dogs
Is that women don't chase motorbikes." And off he went

To *The Turk's Head*. The man
In the pitch-pine raft gesturing to the sky *Here We Go!*
Which is the unexamined and unbeknownst exuberance of one
About to disappear smoothly over a waterfall still bursting
With all he has to say to the one he wrongly thinks he knows,
Looking on coolly from the bank. As he strode along the suburban
Streets he imaged his and Pete's concordance on the *Daniel* book
Clicking tightly as Lego bricks before two-thirds
Of his first pint had been consumed,
Then broadening into the Tinniswood world itself:
The joy of small-and-dour, the equation of impossible dreams of escape
With a gaily-painted gypsy life, and the equation beneath the equation –
Impossible dreams and romance. But when it came

To the putative rejuvenating powers of neonates, he didn't have a baldy;
Though what a pancake stack of questions he had for Pete. It was
A Wednesday and Pete was always there on a Wednesday and, come
To think of it, he was there on all other days too. Belmont waited
With fizzy water, the book before him now suddenly 'this silly book'
To him. He knew already what would never happen any more but
He returned two further days, finally asking the barman if he knew
What happened to the chap I used to drink with and, *yes of course,*
Of course, the barman said he couldn't remember him drinking
With anybody: "Just you reading a grey hardback
Over a couple of pints."

20. Song of the Softening Head

Told this, he lolled in dead air.
He arranged the satchel of the experience
And took himself off. He impersonated himself
As an unaltered master of wry realism,
Keeping the self that had stepped into
This airy zone as a fantasy friend to be embraced later.
He looked

At it this way: the story of PT (he now called him) and himself
Was living proof of the mirror world in which babies
Could rejuvenate oldsters. If there can be one
Then there can be the other. The landscape

Touched on before
Could be a grim place: substations, barbed wire, ruts, motorways,
Cow-shit, dog-shit. But who said he had to pass along it?
There is a landscape of clouds above that, more interestingly
Coloured, silent, full of aspiration and dominance. He
Would live in this hopeful place that his 3 a.m. self said was
'Soft in the Head Land'.

Then, softening into another semi-dream
In the prickly heat of his single bed:
Here is the shadow-world where one dead
And distrustful of glory, a deflation-bard
Walked booted on the Earth.
He'd pulled back the black-marble coverlet of his bed
And travelled down to share the afternoon light with Belmont;
A man too gentle for scepticism,
Too ravening for scepticism.
So take your pick:
His 'afterglow,' his 'residue',
His keeping what he thought the dead knew.

21. Are You "Scotty" or "Spotty"?

If you were on the coast at this point you would see
The sea was purple and the sky black.
Thunder rolled and then spasmed and around *chez* Thom.
The air was so thick you could cut it like cake.
Tuppence sat at the dining table supporting her head
As if it were a cannon ball, saying over and over,
"The bastards! The bastards!"
Had one of her patronees failed to bring it to fruition?
Was the current crop of applicants to *The Tuppence Thom Prize*
For Innovative Art not up to scratch?
No. The psychopathic killer in a popular TV drama
Had been given the name Villanelle. What she'd thought
Was her daughter's unique – yes *unique* – name
Was now a commonplace "in some or other bollocks."
"If only

She'd been a boy," said Belmont. "I'd bet good money you'd
Have been safe with *Pantoum*."
"Still joking, Jokerman! Thought you'd given that up.
Now off you pop … The coinage has been debased,"
She said as the telephone rang in the hall.
"That'll be for you Bellboy. Nobody rings my landline.
Now off you waddle and answer it."

"Daddy? I've got some news."
"I know. Mum's cursing to high heaven in the dining room."
"What? Don't be silly …
You're going to be a grandfather. I'm going to deliver in early January
And we know it'll be a boy.
So you'll be a granddad.
Isn't that fanTASTic!"

He held the receiver away from his face and he cried.
He cried nearly as much as Villy's Lee would cry when told a joke
By a ten-year-old.
Tears of joy and confusion, pure but confined joy.
And tears of release.

Maybe released to fall, and you don't know if it's down
A rabbit-hole, or a lift-shaft, or whether
Your tears of whatever will drown or not drown
The small and precious of your little trip.
There are pigeonholes as you fall past, blurred
So you cannot see their labels, though you know
They dignify the scene.
In a few blessèd seconds you'll be free from the upper story,
Made of wires woven between science journals
And pop-songs, pub evenings and missed breakfasts.
You could land on greasy concrete, or worse:
You could land in an East End pie-and-mash shop,
Where David and Brooklyn Beckham are carefully and smilingly
Eating in their identical flat caps. It's meaningless, quite,

But isn't meaninglessness what you need right now –
When meaning is pressing on you like the converging
Walls of a fatal ante-room, as enjoyed
At the Saturday morning pictures?
'Look Scotty – or is it Spotty? – there's a high window
And here to hand a handy steel bench or beam'. Escape
Is what's mandated, not mere release, something
If not with continuous aspect,
At least with the long-lasting legacy from a cause.
A few minutes later

        Belmont was walking into the dining room
With the words: "In January, my dear, you will be a granny.
To a boy.

Way to go granny."
"No! Without consulting me? I'm too young
To be a grandmother."
"I'd better text her some possible names."

22. This Lunar Beauty Has Some History

Hyacinth
[*After the hero of the only Henry James novel that Belmont
had been able to get through. The first suggestion in a list of boy's
names that Villy had asked her dad for. This particular list
was the 'too feminine or silly' one.*]
Precious
Leslie
Jobriath
[*The failed American Bowie*]
Jean
Daniel
Lassie
Pudeen
Verone
Booty
Holly

And later the 'too macho or silly' one:

Tucker
[*After the Fox News nut-job*]
Porter
[*after Mr Waggoner*]
Carter
[*after the young un-professional in* Daniel]
Brick
[*after the Tin Roof unfortunate*]
Biff
Jet
Daniel
Dogg
Bear
Spear
Yes-Way

Finally, after no whiff of success, he sent in desperation:

Mick-Keith
Charlie-Bill
Brian-Mick
Pantoum
DANIEL Whoops! Cap-lock problEMS.

Belmont knew she'd know it was a joke,
But also that he was serious about Daniel. She could
Not be directed,
Only ironically nudged.
But biting she was not. She emailed:
'We've gone for Porter, daddy, sorreeee!
It's very original.
We'd never have come up with it without you.
Why not pop up and see us?
We need nursery advice'.

He went up, jumping at the chance. As soon as
The taxi delivered him into the landscape
Of Villy and Lee's slice of suburbia
And deposited him outside
Their huge mock-Tudor façade.
He felt more at home than when at home.

Most suburbia is flat, but this was not.
Proud chunky edifices crested hillocks
Of garden stone to say:
Here's my castle, wanna make anything of it?
I mean, they said this to Belmont, whose ideal
Home was a bolthole, and who saw it as
Bad taste to make a home apparent
(Like making the lavatory an architectural centrepiece).

Once there he did what he always did:
Cooked, as Villy was more of an eater than a cook

And the thought of Lee cooking was dangerous/hilarious;
Got lost on his afternoon walks
Because all the Lanes and Meads and Granges
And Walks and Knowles and Drives and Meadows
Looked the same,
Being as featureless as the moon to him,
And, given the ash-grey of the rock gardens
And of the paths leading up to the baronial doors,
A similar colour. It was lunar too
In that the locals seemed to stay indoors
Like Clangers in their burrows. He
Watched TV, which they did no matter what was on –
Lee and Belmont with a beer
And Villy marking Physics problems with one hand
And grabbling handfuls of Bombay mix with the other.
He watched her eyes flick from screen to paper-sheaf
To snack, search-light-style. Their main project

                              was the nursery, about which Belmont
Did indeed advise and which he painted all day long,
Wallowing in Radios 4 and 4-Extra.
Christ how dull?
Or not?
Is peace dull?
Yes, wonderfully, gorgeously dull. Going out

With Lee on his pub-florist rounds certainly
Was not dull. Lee's talk devoured the day.
Cut up with, "All-well-Profs? Alright-Profs?
And Nearly-there-Profs." He would turn up
In an open-truck chocka with hanging baskets,
Impossibly identical: flowers white, pink, red –
That Lee called "lobelias" and Belmont knew were not.
At the pubs
Lee's hanging them and giving them a cursory water
Took almost no time, but the confab between him
And the landlord was an intense affair – at least at first.

Lee would bring with him, and into the pub's back room,
A flight-bag he'd lock and unlock with weird seriousness,
Shielding the combination from the man he would introduce as
'Me dad-in-law'.
Eventually the two men would emerge
And the landlord would say,
"Right dad-in-law, what'll it be?"
They both looked relieved and Belmont
Looked suspicious until
He'd finished his large Jack Daniels on the rocks.
He told himself that only in *The Archers* was it
Inevitable that a shady activity would be punished,
Plus the hideous familial knock-on.

He put his suspicions on his Jack ice and loved
The further being
Of Porter Belmont Fear (yes *Fear*).
The newly night-owl Belmont would lean out
Of his bedroom window, relishing the doubly-
Lunar landscape under sodium light, knowing
This to be ideal terrain
For the space-landing he longed for.

23. Less Sicklied O'er with the Pale Cast of Glym?

Belmont woke up the next day feeling no different.
He didn't *think* he did ...
By 'the next day', I mean January the 7th – with four now in the lunar house –
The three, plus little Porter, whom
Villy called Porty and Lee called PBF.

The day before PBF had lain along Belmont's legs
With his head on his granddad's knees. So trusting, he thought
The parents, to let this absent-minded man do this. What
If he'd suddenly stood up to answer the phone or
Arched to scratch his backside? ...
But of course you don't, do you?
The baby mostly slept.
Belmont put his index fingers into PBF's palms
And felt and saw a strong grasping reflex.
He tried the Moro reflex by touching the cheek
To see if the baby would turn to that side ... much weaker:
As if this intelligent boy
Would have truck with sham nipple.
Mostly,
He had forgotten the *Daniel* scenario or dream as he watched for that
Distinctive smile, like neither mum's nor dad's but a lot like
That of Anthony Head, the actor who'd found fame as one half
Of the *Gold Blend* coffee advert on TV. Think
Of the ironical sucking of a sherbet lemon.

But *some* of the time he did live in the hope of *Daniel*-like powers,
Feeling out for rejuvenating waves, a deepening of the voice,
A general perking up of the limbs and mind.
But nothing.
The boy was lovely and healthy and that was enough.
Tuppence?

She'd kept the birth quiet from her courtiers and from
Her flotsam penumbra, merely grimacing
When Belmont called her granny, saying she'd 'pop up'
When her 'mad' schedule of meetings began to 'ease off'.

But here was the morning after. Yes, he did feel a little more rested than usual.
He got up.
Did his knees creak a little less? And didn't
The soles of his feet usually feel tender on the floor first thing?
Did he not usually feel the need to insert his hearing aids
To get the beauty of the *Today* programme loud?
The contours and content of his face in the bathroom mirror …
Still as aged as ever. But there was something only its
One careful owner could appreciate.
Let's put it this way: Thomas Hardy

Had a genius for the sentence or phrase of killing pith, one that could
Carry the weight of a decent poem.
The face of the young Glym Yeobright
Had a 'beauty', but one that would eventually
Be 'ruthlessly overrun by its parasite thought',
Of course, Belmont's face had aged,
But more to the owner's eye was this *overrunning*
Visible in the eyes themselves (mainly the left)
And in the lines around the mouth.
A souring of cognitive froth, like hangover souring.
He was hung-over from years of the parasite thought
Of cracking hard nuts in his mind.
But today, the 7th of January, the sour froth
Was being sucked back by an outgoing tide.
And this – God help us –

Fed the parasite in turn:
How did he know that this
Did not result from

The simple joy his grandson brought?

Bring on my cavalry of science and scepticism, he told himself.

But ...

He would "bet good money" (his codger phrase)

It was more than this. He'd bet

Good money on magic.

24. The Ninny World without Belmont

The next morning (the last of his stay)
Was much the same, but more so,
And his hopeful belief hardened to certainty.
Villy said, "My God daddy, you do look revived."
Lee said, "You been using that hair-thickening shampoo, Prof?"
Villy said, "Nice shiny cheeks. Must be the wind up here."
Lee said (poking gentle fun at his father-in-law's Dylan tastes), "Shinin'
        Like a mornin' star, Prof." And laughed his boots off.
Belmont said, "I'll be back soon," and meant it. He knew
He couldn't stand more than a few days
Back at Camp Tuppence.

Many years ago they'd gone to a German expressionist play,
The action of which took place in a bourgeois living room.
An unusual feature of which was a figure in the corner
Swaddled as thoroughly as the Invisible Man
In bloody bandages,
But with evident padding: needed because
As the actors passed it – called *Der Schlutz* or
Der Schmultz or *Der Schlumz* or, never mind –
They would punch and kick it to the floor.
Having given up wishing the thing would hit back,
Belmont read in the programme that *Der Schlumts*
Or *Der Schkranz* or *Der Schmutz* symbolised the German colonies
Prior to WWI ... Well, he's now had enough of being *Der Schwatzit*
At Camp Tuppence. The padding

                had more or less gone and now, post Porter,
The name-calling
Hit bone. The courtiers' distain
Nudged a fresh quantum of hot rage in Belmont.

"I'm going to write a book," lied he.

"And the upshot is?" said she.

"Just that there's too much er *activity* here, so I think
    I'll go up to Villy's for an extended..."

"Yes, very quiet there," said she, "lots of peace as the baby
    cries all night."

"It's peaceful in other ways. Better than your flotsam yacking
    through the night, playing horrible music, getting
    in my way in the kitchen."

"My *flotsam*!"

"Or – if you like – your parasites, your piss-artists."

"Any more beginning with 'p'?"

"Your posturing ninnies."

"Oh poor Bellboy."

"Don't you *ever ever* call me that again."

.

.

,

,

"What's the book about?"

"Ah now, there you have me."

"No, really. What's it about?"

"The neglect of the objective, scientific attitude
    in – what your posturing ninnies call –
    the national conversation. It will be called
    The World without the Mind."

[*In fact, this was a book he would secretly love to write; yes
this man who thought that the ghost of Peter Tinniswood
with whom he established a boozy rapport had vouchsafed
to him a simple means by which one could ...*
"*turn back TAHAM*" *and* "*find UHU WAHAY*" *to what ...
he'd get back to you on that*].

As she pretended to laugh he called Villy and gave her the same story.

"Wonderful daddy. How exciting! Come soonest ... "

He thought Tuppence would be pleased to see the back of him,
But she was angrily wounded – seemed to be. Her barbs were
Quite desperate, never following-through.
"Pack your medications in a tea-chest, Belmont
And I'll send them on up to you by Group 4 Securicor."
"I'll register with a GP up there."
"Oh no you won't."

25. It Would Take a Second E. J. Thribb to...

To dream the impossible dream ...
Belmont did so most nights in this exciting limbo.
He could not dream of a squared circle or a perpetual motion machine
But he could dream of a chimpanzee orchestra
Playing *Das Lied von der Erde* behind two human singers.
Look, there's one chimp leaning a little forward to play
A delicate *cor anglais* passage, and check out
The chimp on the harp.
Instead of taking a collective bow, they all run off
During the applause in different directions,
Out to jump on the roofs of taxis waiting around the Albert Hall,
Or to swarm up the Albert Memorial. Impossibility

Was Belmont's new element, his new wide sea.
Was it possible, he thought as he
Sipped his coffee in carriage 'D' of the northbound train
And pushed back his codger's straw hat and set it behind his firm quiff,
For the travelling circus around him to explode into *Oklahoma* song?
"Possible to take a solo?"
"Oh what a beautiful latte!"
He'd brought his laptop for pretend typing.
He'd brought (for reasons
To emerge) a supply of sugar pills a colleague had had
Left over from a placebo group ...
Yes, it *will* emerge that the impossible happened
And its prefiguration had been just that. As he arrived

              at the lunar house he saw Lee
Loading a suitcase and his all-important flight-bag
Into the boot of his car. "Just off down to Wales
For a few days, Prof, to check out some pub-flower growers

For the business. See you in ten."
"Ten minutes?"
"Ten days, Prof. Catch as catch can!" (his version of catch you later).
And so for the next ten days the rocking-to-sleep
And general minding fell to granddad, who every morning
Awoke to a new Oklahoma surge. The comic genius

Of Peter Cook was clear to see
In his "E. J. Thribb (17 and-a-half)" poems; and when
He died their magic was gone.
I need to explain …
E. J. Thribb, in the magazine *Private Eye,* specialises
In poems as funeral orations beginning:
So farewell then.
Well,
I would like to launch a new Thribbism:
It would take a second X, which, I am not, to…
Right now it would need to be
It would take a second Ovid, which, I am not, to
Capture the metamorphosis of Belmont
And so much the better if it could have
Some Ted Hughes sauce.
But I'm not up to it.
Neither, as will emerge later, up to being
A second Sophocles or Homer to capture
Events-in their-modes distortedly mirrored.

Ovid was, in my defence, provided with fast, exciting
Changes (beautiful women into trees or birds,
The drama of bark for skin and sudden feathers
On your arms, talons for hands),
The facts themselves do so much work. But here it was:
A matter of quanta, of creepings forward. Gaining
Hair can be as exciting as losing it.

26. Sugar in the Morning, Sugar in the Evening ... *Fahrkin'!*

What might Ovid have done with these?

→ Not needing to get up to pee multiple times in the night
→ Negligible nose and ear hair
→ Negligible love handles and a flatter belly
→ Feeling light and flexible
→ And physically stronger even
→ Not struggling for proper names and bog-standard
                              "open class" words
→ Regularly thinking of undressing women (deliberate ambiguity)
→ Elaborations of the above
→ Wanting to get on and do things (see immediately above)
→ Regaining hair and original hair colour
→ Face lines melting down into fresh smoothness
          like fork-traces in custard? ... Yes with *Belmonte,*
                    vanishing cream available from all good pubs
→ Bursts of silly-singing, such as inserting a loud cowboy YEE HA!
          into sensitive ballads like *Homeward Bound* and
                    The Look of Love

And this was after only nine days ... a 'wonder'.

"Daddy I'm really worried now. This is scary!"
Belmont told Villy the following: he had 'with Ron Haworth from
Physiology' (an invention) managed to devise a formula
That not only arrests,
But reverses ageing. He had volunteered to try on himself what had
So successfully been done to rats ... Then it was just a matter of further
Clinical trials and then waiting for the call from Stockholm. "Look,
Here are the pills [sugar ones, recall] I have to take – one in the

Morning, one in the evening." At which point he thought back to the PT
Afternoons, in which at one point they did a whispered rendition
Of a pretend-drunk Jimmy James singing Alma Cogan's
Sugar in the Morning, Sugar in the Evening, Sugar at
Supperrrr Time.

Now, as I said: Villy was credulous; but she wasn't stupid.
"Arresting ageing I can get. But reversing the ageing process.
Nobody can beat entropy Dad!"
"Can you trust me on this darling? That's all
I can say, *Can* you?" (he found himself channelling Claire Rayner).
She did not trust him on it, knew it was fishy but
On the surface accepted.
She was cool with him for the first time ever.
Not because she thought he was lying ... well ...
But because she was worried about him.

Belmont hated this. He hated too how 'parasite thought'
Seemed, though leaving fewer traces as it crept
Under his demeanour,
To itself be getting younger and stronger. It made
Him think about what's happening to his brain.
Will it get younger, so he'd lose the precious
Pannier of knowledge (of science and the everyday)
Hanging within it? He knew he could be
An arrogant toad when younger ... Now, I can be sour
And miserable but I'm nicer to people;
Gentler, more patient. Who wants really
To be on this helter-skelter?
On the ground is better.
He was wrapped

In these thoughts in the sitting room, keeping their
Rhythm by jiggling his leg in energy overflow
When he heard Lee's voice in the kitchen.

He was back, back through the kitchen door. Lee had
Planned to say to Belmont, with Villy's agreement,
Roughly this:
"Hi there, Prof. Yep I'm back. Wales was as lovely as ever.
Tell you what, Prof., Vill has just informed me that she thinks
There's a leak of something coming down from the loft
Into our bedroom, so we're going up there for a bit
To try to sort it.
Do you think you could keep an ear out for PBF?
We'll be about, say, half an hour – give or take."

But what he actually said was:
"Stroll on! Fahrkin stroll ON."

27. George Bernie Schwartz is Trimmed

In Belmont's beloved phrase *the world without the mind,*
There is nothing in common between a *good book,* a *good*
Chicken and a *good fight.* Doesn't there have to be
Some filling up with the rubble of circumstance, some
Prototypes, some particulars? A *good holiday?*
Now let me see …
Wearing a handkerchief knotted at the corners for a hat,
Unending strong sun, yellow sand, solid blue sky;
"dips" with the rest of the crowd in the sea; outside
The guesthouse only ice-cream and chips to eat, only
Beer to drink; your peers are bossy fat women
And their shrivelled husbands walking six paces behind;
Blondes in bikinis with breasts like torpedos, cheeky boys;
Inside the guesthouse (when admitted after 5pm), there's
Cleanliness and plain nourishing food and it's easy to ignore
The old geezer in the corner telling us all he cannot eat tomato
Skins because he only has half a stomach. What kind

of lunatic would say this would be good for more than a day?
Likewise, the Belmont case. Here was a holiday of good things:
Doing only what was expected of him, being with his daughter,
The cooling lunar landscape in which Lee was a moon man.
You could say his role was feminine – cooking, baby-minding,
Bit of tidying up, and against this, Lee's exercise room
With its resistance machines and static bike that addicted him.
But only a lunatic … He was a beefy
Embarrassment and a hairy one too, not cutting his hair or beard
In a dopey attempt to disguise his youthfulness. Lee's eyes
Had a dimmer light at the sight of him, and Villy was often on the point
Of welling up.

Tuppence was too busy to visit this 'cultural desert', so they took
The baby down to see her, leaving Belmont treading water.
He couldn't leave the house and if he was glimpsed the story
Was he was a visiting friend. Imagine now – this is poem
Enough (recall the sub-prose kind touched on before)
To leave it to the readers to do their bit and imagine
What this was like for him. Anything you come up with
Will be just the ticket. Mostly
Belmont read and kept his young-looking nose clean.

Little Porter melted his grandmother's heart, but
Things were not well *chez* Tuppence.
"Mum's life isn't her own, dad.
The word has gone around that you two split up.
There are all these creepy men hanging about."
"There always were, Villy."
"No, it's worse now. They're older and straighter.
They're eating her out of house and home.
There's this sleazy guy in a blazer and cravat
Who keeps coming round for help with his bloody poems,
And he winks at her.
They've got their eyes on her money, I'd say."

To their huge surprise,
What Belmont said to this was:
"Lee, do you think you could arrange for somebody
To come round and cut my hair, trim my beard.
Oh and Villy, maybe you could buy me some new clothes."

An ancient, confused cutter came from one of the flowery pubs.
"I think," said Belmont, "I'll go for a clean-cut look.
I look like George Bernard Shaw right now."
"You want a Tony Curtis you mean?"
"No."
"Wasn't George Bernie Shaw his real name?"

… Belmont ponders: "Bernard *Schwartz* I think.
But yes, a Tony Curtis with short back and sides
And a neat beard please." He looked, in the end,
Like something between a 1950's geography teacher
And a judgemental gym bunny.

That evening Porter looked hard at Belmont,
Then looked at his mum, then back to Belmont
And said "Gadah!" as if to say, "you can't fool me" …
"He's just said his first word daddy – *granddad*."
Next morning, there was not a trace of Oklahoma surge.
Porter was no longer, no longer strictly, a baby,
And a dark purpose dawned.

28. Grime, Grimace and Genre Defiance

This is how the helter-skelter is grounded:
On a pavement outside a station
Before one's 'black branch' of choice.
He felt quite other but this other was no hero.
Actions – one can blog – don't sit
On a continuum between good and bad but on one
Between easy and difficult. Difficult? Bravery
And doing things for others at a cost to oneself.
It's the difficulty, not the goodness, that's marked.

This is easy: making mischief. Science was easy for him.
Suffering his wife was easy as he had the capacity. Now,
Here he is selecting a branch for what kind of mischief
To go in for. Within
A narrative shape, the ground is sequestered, cutting
What can be said down to its own size; while abstractions
Are flavourless. If only the right abstraction could gain
Narrative nourishment, while the narrative allows itself
To rattle off its chains in an abstract cloud. Fat chance

In his present singleness of purpose.
With his field of vision 360 degrees but 6 feet in diameter,
Here were the familiar but unfamiliar streets and his blood
Was beating a tattoo in his young unaided ears.
And he was at his own front door.
No need to ring. The door was ajar.
"You for the sculpture committee?" (a sloppy Joe enquired).
"Just looking for TT."
"Artist?"
"Playwright."
"Grab some dinner and I'll let her know you're here."

The dining room was set up for a meeting and the rest
Of the house was a dining room. Here again
Was Ivor Cutler's plum-tree sucking taste-treats
Through its greedy roots. In what used to be
His study a small group was passing round a joint.
He'd always hated the word 'munchies' and here they were:
The fruits of the deli-counter and a huge box of chocolates,
All back-grounded by music that was hip-hop or trip-hop
Or grime or grimace. Elsewhere,
People swigged fine wines and tucked right in.

He passed a room where Tuppence was before a laptop
With another. Helping a neophyte to polish a sonnet? No,
Making an Ocado order as directed by
The creepy blazered one, who spoke:
"Maybe three bottles of Remy Martin, a dozen Bordeaux,
cheese ... now, let me see. Beef Wellingtons certainly."
When finished, they addressed Blazer's latest poem;
She helping him to decide between 'a zeitgeist',
'the zeitgeist' and 'that zeitgeist' ... Later,
in the kitchen, a dodderer was removing a chicken
from the oven and directing a potato salad. He
withdrew again ...
"Ah, a new face" (He'd just bumped into his wife).
"Don't tell me ... Novelist?"
"Playwright."
"Come."
She took him by the hand and led him into a quietish corner,
Where Tuppence's eyes had a light he'd not seen for many years.

Belmont told her he was re-working Tinniswood's sitcom
I Didn't Know You Cared about the Brandon family, but
With all the comedy drained and nastiness put in its place.
He was, you see, darkening it to symbolise the dark times
In which we live.

Uncle Mort is now a paedophile, Brandon Carter a drug dealer,
His wife a whore.
"I've called it *Actually, we Don't Care.*
I really don't know whether to think of it as genre-defying
Or as inaugeerating," – Belmont affected a south London drawl
And lugubrious stupidity – "a new genre that I call
Sit-trag, if you gets my drift.
In the episode I've just written Carter runs over
And kills his mother and steals cheese and cream crackers
From her shopping bag. As I see it,
We're now in the zone of post-comedy.
Nothing is funny no more, Mrs Thom."
"Oh, 'Tuppence' please."

29. Shit and The Widow

Remember the 'black branch'?
The poet says, 'it is our support
And control, what we do with life in
The phase now running on'.
I can't say I know what that is meant to mean,
Though I can make sense of it. Textual evidence
Suggests he had in mind how the colour black
Absorbs and so *retains* colour. Here in the phase
Now running on there were brilliant colours –
His youth and vigour and rebel cheek, his wife lusting
After him, and that there was something building and
About to breech in drama colours: purples and oxbloods
Thrown against a white wall. But it was not

                reflected onto the peopled world.
It was retained within the "sit-trag" unfolding
In the small branching nodes of choice.
As darkness fell
The slum of the scene was, for him, late-night opening
At the Cordoba mosque on mescal.
Time advanced and some bodies left. A zombie
Offered them flutes of Prosecco and she said,
"We can do better than this," and fetched
A bottle of *Veuve Clinquot.*
"Is that the one day call The Widow?"
"Yes. Anyway, it makes me feel like the merry widow."

Usually she drank little and if she did it was either champagne
Or Guinness, so he whispered to the zombie
(Having routed himself down one nodal branch)
To fetch some Guinness. And they drank
As they tucked into the chicken commandeered
From the dodderer.

This Tom-Jones chicken scene was spied upon
By the creepy brethren and the Blazer was crestfallen
In con-fab with other oldie suitor-gluttons.
In his youth Belmont had, and now
Had again, something
Of the Albert Finney about him.
And this he displayed in the sideways brazen of his chewing,
Regal gestures of bone disposal, and a Tuppence-directed twinkle.
He'd found one of her hairbrushes in the loo
And with it he elevated his quiff. This
Was living.
And here was the lull, when the drink turned bad
For the others and good for them …
"Do you know what you're up to?" he said to himself.
"In the short term, yes; in the long, nobody knows,"
Was his reply.

Now, who would dwell on the female body revealed
In the throw-and shawl-rich perfumed bedroom?
Or on her smiling at her own good luck
As the male undressed?
What *was* there of this wife in the woman
He was about to make love to?
Not the face, and that body for so long
Unvisited by him was   well, it was
Tuppence. He was happy.
And who would dwell on the actions except to say
That when they had finished their conditions
Could be described as satisfactory.

30. My Name's Tim Streatfield. Whaaat's YOURRS?

He'd told her his name was Tim Streatfield
Was his first thought on waking.
"Tim … Tim … Are you awake darling?"

He was black. He had retained all the Cordoba colours
Of the booze and that along with his memory of the night
Made him as black as death. What a way to find out
That your wife had been unfaithful to you!
In a voice he feared might have some Old Poison
In it he gave his sadistic breakfast order.
"*Café con leche* … very strong espresso and warm not boiled
Milk. Two boiled eggs, slightly soft in the middle,
Thinly sliced, served on sourdough or rye-bread toast
Spread liberally with unsalted butter,
Finished with ground white pepper and a little salt."

"Yes, *Sir*."

His blackness was building all the time it took for this
To be prepared. Below she was shooing flotsam
Out of the kitchen, fluttering and chattering like a school-girl.
And it kept building till the food arrived and was handed to him …

"Cor, thanks mum."

She looked hard at him.

"How is it Tim?"

"Great thanks mum. Eggs a bit too well done though mum."

"Why do you keep calling me 'mum' like a Dickensian crossing sweeper?"

Belmont put his plate aside and stepped out of bed.

"Look at me. Who do I remind you of?"
"Well I did think you looked a bit like my husband
In his younger days. Why?"

"I should do. He's me dad."

"Mum! [he opened his arms to her]. I'm back
Your son's a bit of a libertine [pronounced leiber-tyne] innee?"

She shielded his face from her. There were no screams.
Not the seizing up with shock. She palmed off the sight
Of him and vanished downstairs where she filled

Buckets with cold water and, like the apprentice in drowning mode,
Emptied them on the heads of all the sleeping figures she could find.
The conscious walking gluttons she told that they had three minutes
To leave before she called the police. Then

It was a if she could see a funny side (she could not) as she repeated
Come on perverts. Off you pop!"
Belmont dressed quickly and stepped out the back door,
Shocked at himself.

31. Stani Acquires Some Football Vocabulary

Here's an indigestible phrase:
Representational solipsism
(Coined by Jerry Fodor).
Meaning what?
That while Jocasta was tormented by a *true* belief
About incestuous coupling and Tuppence was tormented
By a *false* belief about incestuous coupling, there is no reason
To believe their torments differed in intensity.
And after all, Tuppence was no Queen and she had surely
Suffered enough already.

Turning to Belmont in passing:
What is *emotional solipsism*?
(A coining of my own)
Meaning what?
It means that Belmont was furious with his wife
For being unfaithful to him, *despite*
Her doing so with Belmont himself.

But Belmont, himself, can wait till later …

Jocasta was almost a MacGuffin: she advanced
The plot devastatingly by trying to buck the prophesy
Markets. And who can blame her?
Though she was sound about it: 'Better to live and
Let things be'.
She was a good, though corny psychologist: 'Think how many
Men have gone to bed together with their mothers in dreams'.
She was an efficient stoker of the male o-me-*miserum*:
'poor man' … 'man of sorrow'.

But, what do we hear of her sorrow from her lips?
Not a dicky bird.
We're told of her being 'frantic', rushing into her chamber.
We hear her fingers 'were twisted in her hair'
And that she hanged herself. Not so,

       her son-and-lover, who was merely streaked
In the face by 'bloody jelly' and lived
To campaign on the *o-me-miserum* ticket.

Tuppence was a creature, like Jocasta –
Of actions not words.
It was the best Christmas some rough sleepers
Had ever known – waking in doorways to bottles
Of *Chateaunuef du Pape* and huge blackcurrant-topped
Pork pies beside their heads. Then she was off
To food-banks with un-perishable feasts the parasites
Had laid up. She scrubbed and vacuumed. She poured
14-year-old malts down the bog. A couple of hours
Online and all her projects and involvements and follies
were stone dead. Standing orders were fish in a barrel.
She changed her email address and mobile number and
Listened for the front door-bell like a gladiator …

Brrrring!
"Oh hi, TT."
It would give me pleasure to report the short sharp verbal
Shocks she delivered, having planned them to a T.
But again, you can imagine them. Their words were
The usual suspects.
As for Blazer, she simply gave him a short sharp shove:
Leaving him upended like a tortoise at the bottom
Of her five-step walk-up. Then …

Brrrring!
"Right, another one of the bastards."

But it was a petite, pretty young woman with her hair in a bun
And a young boy beside her: her cleaner, Maya
And her son, Stani who was over here for Christmas
From Bulgaria.
Now this was the mark of the new Tuppence. She,
Who never bit her tongue, now thought this but did not
Say it about this woman and her ten-year-old:
'What a way to live. To give up a decent job, to leave
Your son with your mother to come over here to clean
Other people's houses.
A boy needs his mother.
He's there and you're here trying out restaurants.
Bulgaria must be fucking *awful* to be worse than
England is right now.
Bring him here and if you can't: go back and live with him.
The thought-phrase 'go back' shocking herself … '
But she smiled and said, "Oh sorry, I forgot it was Wednesday."

She sat the boy beside her, turning on the TV, found a football
Match and worked on his vocabulary.
"That is called *a foul.*"
"Foal."
"No *foul.*"

And when they had gone, three hours later, she washes
The curtains and worked on the neglected garden.
Yes, there were chinks of black light though the armour,
But suppression this was not repression: she knew
What she was doing. This was one of the 'difficult'
Things I blogged about before. It took all her strength.
Don't ask me

About her face. Some of the work was not reversible.
Some was and so it was a matter of not attending clinics
Where she was punctured and tightened up. The whiteness
Of her hair began as a skunk stripe
And widened like a smile.

32. Behind the Chain-set and into the Trees

A sunny Sunday on the tow-path with families,
Some weird loiterers and then approaching from front or rear,
Husband and wife cyclists; husband first, lycra-ed,
Goggled like Lance Armstrong travelling very quickly
And unswervingly, sounding bells or horns and shouting,
"scuse me" and making people jump aside tasting
adrenaline and curses. Well …

Here is an oldster with a walking stick and a scorpion
Fire in his eyes. He removes the ferule from the stick
And just as hubby rides past, he stabs the stick
Matador-style
Into the back wheel, just behind the chain-set.

It was not only anger at his wife and at himself that made
Belmont do the 'mum' routine. It was exactly in the spirit
Of the bike-stabber. Yes, hubby might career to one side
And brain a toddler, yes one of the weird loiterers
Might get the crook of a walking stick in his balls at an acute
Angle and 20 miles an hour. But, more likely, hubby would skid
Into the canal. All being well, he would struggle to disengage
His feet from their bijou pedal housings and may nearly drown.
Yes, he may drown in fact; but wouldn't the *Thought for Today*
Just write itself? On the whole,

It would have been well done. It would result in
Humility deliverance. And even if no humility at all
Were delivered. Well,
Sometimes things have just got to be buggered up.
Not to some good or further purpose.
Just buggered up.

33. Hit the North!

In the landscape of this,
Husband and wife were light years apart.
And so, as in an Einstein thought-experiment,
We cannot talk about the times in which they aged
As being equivalent, as being within the same overarching time:
They were different envelopes of time in different mental worlds.

Belmont was settling down.
He was welcoming back an old friend.
When the taxi dropped him off later that day
In the lunar landscape that he had grown to love
He deeply breathed the fresher colder air, strolled
About for a bit thinking of the hilly landscape traversed
Between there and here and noted with satisfaction his limp

Knocking on the door
Of his left leg. He felt as if
About to fall into a delicious sleep.
Tuppence, meanwhile, bustled about herself
Like a harassed caretaker. She was not relaxed
About what her mirror was beginning to show, feeling
As she did, or thought she did, to be 'a little over forty'.

But, as ever,
She just got on
With things. Things?
Volunteering at the Marie Curie
Shop, refurnishing her house, teaching
Herself how to garden. Here was Nature
She could impose her will on. She thought she didn't

Feel lonely,
But she did in fact.
Villy was about the happiest
She had ever been; Porty rampant;
And her dad slowly but surely coming back.
She almost cheered when he *lowered* himself
Into a chair, loved to see his face lined up in the morning.

She only turned away
From this happiness to lecture
Lee on why, no, he should not offer
To buy some of those pills from Belmont.
Belmont had foreseen this possibility, having
His answer ready that 'they are dangerous for
Diabetics, so better not Lee, if you don't mind mate'.

34. In short ...

                        the cyclist
Was dripping on the tow-path
Chastened, wondering what app
He'd need to expedite a power stroll.
Resigned about his £4,000 bike at the bottom
Of the canal, failing to banter back at the passing
Sunday people in their Sunday trainers, strolling on.

35. Porter Floors a Plate or Six

Belmont was deep in thought
Over his pint.
He liked ordering sausage and mash in pubs,
But in some of them they overdid
The onion gravy into a gloop soup.
So, maybe play safe with some gastro experiment
(Sherry-marinated kidney risotto with elderflower
and cherry foam
With a side of quadruplely fried sweet potato),
Which he could enjoy rubbishing. And as for Tuppence
(still bird-motioned, bird-boned and quick),
Chattering on the 'exceptional' development
Of her grandson, she settled on a Caesar salad
And fizzy water. They looked much the same
Age, though at certain angles she seemed
Caught the side-draft from a wind tunnel.

It was spring, and Villy had pulled out all the stops
(Their stops of fear) to arrange a pub lunch
On neutral territory (somewhere in Warwickshire).
Porter presided at the head of the table, banging
On his high-chair table and launching objects to the floor.

There was hope: he agreed with her often (though
Not really); she laughed at his deflating asides; she warmed
Up after a cold pint of Guinness and could even be teased.
While Lee went to the bar and Villy tried to
Clean up Porter they had a whisper, which resulted
At the end in these words from her:
"Well you'd better come back with me, you miserable
Bugger. I've got some jobs for you in the garden."

36. Some Waves

Yes, we know that in autumn
Everything is 'half-dead'
But it's also half-alive.

You crest a hill and there's the sea before you,
Wide open to what you can think of it.
How could the music in your ears compete
With this: the continuous bringing of the news
To which you are addicted? You rip

The headphones off and there you are
In the wind.
You feel free.

But your under-sense of this
Is as a meat safe with great bleeding cuts of meaning
And remembered darkness
That you will mull over until they're broiled
Into raggy chunks. Every sentence you think
Is garaged neatly; and as much as you
Try to wrench the steering wheel away from yourself
Into other avenues, or maybe with a sharp
Left onto the Amalfi coast with bandaged penguins,
You end up high and dry as dust.

Why not just be content with that?
Quick, put the headphones back on
Before the memories in which you star
Start shouting in your ears ...
Try getting a LARF out of that. Try
Being as happy as a pig in iron.

We will now sing Hymn number 64:
I Should Be So Lucky.

37. On the Question of Arse Possession

"How's it going?"
"Good thanks."
Belmont and Tuppence were not quite Darby and Joan,
But they were 'good' in this sense: fine, okay.
With a side order of triple-fried contentment.

She'd caught down with him, who was relieved
He'd stopped the rapid ageing at the point
just before the Porter touch.

It was difficult too.
How they conversed
In the very small intersect of their interests
That throbbed only when the Superbabe came up.
Bickering was dangerous,
Dangerous as a dip-stick into the 'remembered darkness'
Of my little sermon.

Tuppence hinted she was open to the idea
Of sharing a bed,
But he refused to imagine how he would measure against
The 'leiber-tyne' who had last been there. That said,
When they sank a couple of bottles of *Pol Roger*
To celebrate the second birthday of Superbabe
No hints were needed and they stumbled back
Into the dance. It was good (in the above sense),
Or they thought it was – so hard to recall.
But when they drank together again – thanks to
State-dependent memory – it came back,
And as a prospect too.
Good then, though a lot of room for 'better.'
Just after supper one evening the phone rang
And Tuppence answered it.

"Hello, Mrs Thom?" [a mid-Atlantic female voice]
"Yes."
"I have Fraser on the line for you. Please hold."
"Hello … Tuppence Thom?"
"Yes."
"Or should I say 'mother.'"

There was no horror;
Only a long long pause
Because the voice was completely different:
Light, precise, a little Scots and the pushy
Side of smarmy.
"Can you please explain yourself?"
He did.

After this she was white and Belmont held her hand.
"I've just been talking to Junior …
No, it's got to be him from what he knows.
His name is Fraser McBride. 'You've probably heard of me'.
He said. And when I said, 'No', he didn't seem very happy."

He's coming round Friday at 4pm.
Hope that's OK."

They didn't watch much television: recordings of old films,
The News, comedy for Belmont. But the name rang a faint bell
For him.

He's got a series on Channel 4, a series of series called:
So You Think You Have a Something?
On catchup they managed to find an episode each of:
So You Think You Have a Self
So You Think You Have a Memory
So You Think You Have a Conscience.

Each one was a loose series of hints, backed up
With interviews that made a background mosaic
Against which McBride could pose and look
Ironical and sharp and a lot like Zebedee
From *The Magic Roundabout.*

"Do you get Zebedee?" she said.
"Mainly Sammy Davis Junior," he said …
"Innee bold!" he Kenneth Williams-ed.

Each one began with a grey virtual curtain.
Fraser moved in from the right, vanished,
In from the left, vanished,
In from the right again and then his little head
Popped up centre screen to say,
"So You Think You Have a Self."
I say 'moved', not walked, because he glided in
Without leg involvement.
He held his forearms up straight before him,
Parallel to his body, palms facing; and seeing this took Belmont
Back to when his mother would make him
Hold up his hands so she could hang a skein
Of wool between them for her to wind a ball
For knitting. It seemed to mean:
I have special understandings and I am devastatingly
Eccentric and sort of game for a laugh.
To Belmont it suggested he was estimating the width
Of his own head.

A bit of Googling and they saw that he was the 'son'
Of Andrew and Millie McBride, gentry from the
East coast of Scotland. After Fettes, he'd managed
A Third Class in English from Durham. After this
He did more MAs than you could wave a cheque-book at,
Often in the USA.
Some called him a polymath, some a thinker,

Some a neuroscientist and some a provocateur
(No there is no sting in this sentence's tail).
Somehow, he made it into TV via a production
Company daddy owned.
They decided not to watch his TED talk called:
Embrace Your Ignorance.

Friday came.
They were nervous, felt vulnerable and, yes, resenting
Of the intrusion; while thinking maybe what they
Saw was only showbiz and he may turn out
To be a good guy. It may be a shining moment,
May be a life-changer.
But they stayed within the circles of themselves,
Not sharing thoughts about their pop-psychologist son.

A sleek car pulled up and a 'dinky' (this was Belmont
In Tinniswood mode) man emerged from the back,
As did a pretty blonde with a clip-board. She checked
The house. He gave her a goodbye peck on the cheek
And he rang the bell.

"Mum! ... Dad!" he stage-voiced from the threshold.
He gave each of them a very long hug indeed
And wiped a 'tear' from a dry eye.

Yes, Sammy Davis, Belmont thought. Perhaps some
Mr Bojangles might break the ice. But there
Was no ice, only brittle shallow talk
And melt-water sentiment.

They had tea and he asked them if they'd seen
His shows, casting his eyes heavenwards as if to say
'Yes, I'm a star, for my sins'.

"Some of them," they said.

Yes, indeed, he had no interest in his parents at all, no curiosity
About their lives or about his sister.
But his researchers had prepared him so he could say:
"So Belmont, I mean dad, as a leading scientist … " or
"So Tuppence, I mean mum, as a published poet … "

"Well just you wait till the next one:
So You Think You Have Religion."

"Now these are only ideas I'm working on, so
Be gentle with me [grin grin] … Let's give it
A whirl. You may have heard of the pre-frontal
Cortex … you especially dad, the bit of the brain
Responsible for self-control. It goes without saying,
Doesn't it, that it often lets us down. *In itself*
It's not really enough, is it? We need something
Outside of it to complete it functionally.
This, on my conjecture, *is religion* –
The cultural organ or self-control, or
The Exogenous Control Module as I
Dub it … Now,

Have you ever heard of my fellow Scot
Mary Brunton? I'm sure you have mum,
Given your extensive literary nous."

(Still no curiosity about them, need I add).

"You see, despite what they say [drops eyes to floor],
I'm not an *entirely* original thinker and I have
Borrowed ideas from her novel *Self Control,*
Published way back in 1811."

He takes a record card from his wallet.

"This novel was supposed to show (reads)
The power of the religious principle
In bestowing self-command.
Isn't that beautiful?
She gets it. I mean, she got it."

They were mute.

He seemed downhearted by this but then,
As if from a cue he'd generated himself, he said …
"Actually, I may be being a wee bit cheeky here.
But since I tracked you down we've been floating
The possibility of doing
So You Think You Have Parents.

It would be truly wonderful if we could
Work together on this … We would
Reconstruct this very meeting. You'd
Have a chance to get your hair done
(looks at Tuppence). We could bring
in a few bits of interesting furniture, do a photo-
album mock-up.
How about it … er … mum and dad?"

"Absolutely not." [Belmont]

"No, [Tuppence] … but I tell you what:
As you were talking I was getting an idea
For another one you could do:
So You Think You Have an Arse.

Most people have quite nondescript
Self-negating arses. But what about these Kardashian women
With arses like shelves
And weight-lifter men with buns as tight as tight.

You could do *Arses in Literature, Arses*
Down the Ages, The Concept of an Arse.
You could nod away as the Professor of Arse
Studies at Oxbridge University talks in his study.
Oh and I know what … "

"You could play the William Burroughs routine
About the man whose mouth and arse-hole exchange
Functions, so he ends up literally talking
Through his arse."

"A bit like you do, Fraser." [Belmont]

"Oh you must excuse my husband being so direct.
Right though he is."

Well, really [Fraser. Then he tries and fails to laugh].
And I was going to invite you up to Suffolk
To meet my partner."

"Not interested." [Belmont]
"Me neither." [Tuppence]
"Actually [Belmont] we're quite busy now, so if
You'll excuse us.
We need
To wash our feet."

"This is cruel." [Fraser]
"This really is cruel." [in anger more than pain]

Tuppence then adopted a grotesque version
Of her Cleopatra voice, standing up to intone

"You show us a true hell,
It's you who is cruël."

No more was said. He phoned his driver
And the car purred away after some cold farewells.

Husband and wife looked at each other.
There was a pause.
Then they laughed and laughed.
And their love affair began at last.

THE END